Appreciate it!

The Playbook for Employee Recognition

Debra Corey

Cover designed by Leonie Williamson

Typesetting and publishing by UK Book Publishing

www.ukbookpublishing.com

Typeset in Amasis

ISBN: 978-1-915338-08-2

Table of Contents

Introduction

Let me begin this book with a quote that to me sums up so eloquently what appreciation is all about. It's from the wonderful Maya Angelou, who was an American poet and civil rights activist, and who many of us still go to for motivation and inspiration.

"People will forget what you said, people will forget what you did, but people will never forget how you made them feel."

I start here instead of my normal practice of starting with data because I believe that for appreciation to genuinely happen it needs to all start with, as Dr. Angelou says, *a feeling*! It doesn't start with a fancy trophy, a beautiful gift or even money, it starts with a feeling that we matter, that we make a difference, that we're seen, that we belong and that we're appreciated for who we are and what we've done. For no matter who we are, this is something we all need and deserve.

My hope for this book is to change the order, to have companies begin with the feeling, the reason for appreciation, and from here, deliver on this by building their appreciation and recognition programs, their "say and do," around this. Build ones where every employee feels appreciated, not just a few. Build ones where we focus on all of the small things that matter and make a difference, and not just the big ones. Build ones that are "always on" – freely and continuously happening each and every day, and not just every year or every five years. And build ones to create moments and feelings that truly and genuinely matter.

The math and science of appreciation

But why does it matter? Why is it important that we create these moments and feelings, especially through our recognition programs and practices? In the first chapter of this book, I'll answer this question in detail, but I thought it was important to tackle this question from the start, so let me bring in my good friend, "Data," to help me with this, showing how appreciation has statistically and scientifically been proven to drive employee engagement and improve performance.

Let's start with a piece of data from a study[1] that asked employees what matters most to them, and what is the most important thing your manager or company currently does that would cause you to produce great work. The clear winner was appreciation, with 37% of respondents saying "recognize me," higher than getting more pay (7%), getting more training (6%) or getting a promotion (4%), showing how appreciation matters the most to them.

The study also shows that appreciation and recognition matter to our companies, for when answering the question of what matters most to them, respondents also said that by getting more recognition, they'd **produce great work**. Two other studies found similar results, with one[2] reporting that 79% of employees said they'd **work harder** if their efforts were recognized, and another[3] reporting that 82% of employees said that praise and recognition are leading factors in helping them **improve their job performance**. However you slice or report it, the data shows the tangible difference appreciation and recognition can make to a company.

It's not just the data that makes this point, as there is also the science behind the power of appreciation. Studies have shown that when you praise someone your words trigger their hypothalamus, which is a part of the brain that controls eating and sleeping, and a neurotransmitter called dopamine, which has a key role to play in productivity. And that's because when the brain gets triggered to produce more dopamine through appreciation, the dopamine will boost its work and your brain will work at its maximum to do its best. Think of it like chocolate, which also releases dopamine, and how much better you feel (and are) after eating it!

To bring this point to life, let me share a story of when I got multiple dopamine bursts through appreciation. The situation was that I posted

---

1   Study done by Great Places to Work and O.C. Tanner in 2021.
2   Data from Reward Gateway study done in 2017.
3   Data from Gallup study done in 2016.

something on social media to say that I had won an award, something I don't normally do, but I did because the award process had left me feeling negative about the situation and myself. What followed surprised and delighted me, which was that for over a week I received lovely messages in my post to congratulate me and send words of praise. And, you got it, each and every time the dopamine was released and I felt absolutely amazing!

A Little Thanks Goes a Long Way[4]

The good news is that often all it takes is a simple thank you for someone to feel appreciated. A study was conducted that looked at 41 fundraisers responsible for soliciting alumni donations to a university, examining the effects of gratitude on the fundraiser's prosocial behaviors in raising money to benefit the university.

A director visited half of the fundraisers in person, telling them, "I am very grateful for your hard work. We sincerely appreciate your contributions to the university." The second group received no such expressions of gratitude. The results found that the expression of gratitude **increased the number of calls by more than 50%** for the week, while fundraisers who received no thanks made about the same number of calls as the previous week.

"Receiving expressions of gratitude makes us feel a heightened sense of self-worth, and that in turn triggers other helpful behaviors toward both the person we are helping and other people, too," says Francesca Gino, Harvard Business School Professor and Best-Selling Author, in the report. She described the scope of the "gratitude effect" as "the most surprising part" of her research.

It's time for change

The good news is that the positive actions and behaviors described above translate into positive outcomes for our employees and companies too. In fact, according to one study[5], it can lead to two times higher

---

4   Research conducted by Francesca Gino and Adam M. Grant as shared in the Journal of Personality and Social Psychology 2010.

5   Data from O.C. Tanner Institute's 2021 Global Culture study.

revenue, four times more engaged employees, and 43% of employees less likely to suffer burnout. However, and this is a biggie, this only happens when the company has strong recognition programs and recognition cultures.

This leads me to the bad news, which is that although 87%[6] of companies have programs in place to appreciate and recognize their workforce, many are not working. Too many employees **are not being recognized**, with one survey[7] finding that almost seven out of 10 (65%) employees have not been appreciated in the last year, and they **don't feel appreciated**, with another survey[8] finding that almost seven out of 10 (66%) employees do not feel appreciated. Going back to what I said at the start, they may be recognized, but they don't feel appreciated!

The main reason for this is that many companies appreciate their workforce using recognition programs that are stuck in the past, grounded in strategies and methodologies that I was following back when I began in HR over 20 years ago. And it's not just me that thinks this, for one survey[9] found that almost nine out of 10 (87%) employees **feel their recognition program is "stale, outdated, or used as disguised compensation."** If our employees see and say this, then certainly we need to see and address it!

Throughout this book I'll be sharing strategies, tips and examples to help drive new ways of thinking about and designing recognition programs. For recognition to fundamentally change, we need to be the ones who drive that change. Here are six ways I'll cover in the following pages to how we can do just that:

1. We need to move to a more **inclusive approach** to recognition, one where everyone is invited to the party, where we're all treated as individuals, and which drives a sense of belonging through appreciation.

2. We need to move to **recognize the small inputs and contributions** that lead and add up to the ultimate outcome,

---

6   2019 WorldatWork and Maritz Motivation Trends in Recognition report.
7   Study done by Reward Gateway in 2018.
8   Study done by O.C. Tanner in 2017.
9   2021 O.C. Tanner Global Culture Report.

and which keep our people and our work on track and in focus.

3. We need to move to build into our recognition strategies and programs an **understanding of how they are genuinely making employees feel**, removing what I call the "piss off factor," instead driving feelings of appreciation and engagement.

4. We need to make a shift in how we think of and act on appreciation, **giving recognition the starring role** and rewards the supporting one.

5. We need to remove the constraints and guard rails that we've built into our recognition programs that are no longer needed, **giving our people more freedom and autonomy** to give and receive recognition in ways that work for them.

6. We need to **remove the "winner versus loser" mentality** that is ingrained into so many recognition programs, using recognition as a motivator and not as a demotivator.

If change is ever going to happen we need to step out of and step into new ways of looking at and doing recognition. We need to fundamentally readdress **why** we recognize, **what** we recognize and **how** we recognize, challenging traditional ways of thinking and acting.

This book is a starting point to fuel the recognition *rebelution*, one where we rebelliously challenge the status quo of traditional recognition to add the exclamation point to appreciation!

Getting started

Now that I've made my case for change, it's time to move forward and begin our journey together. Here are a few things to know as you get started:

- **Introducing the Recognition Pyramid.**
  For those of you who have read any of my previous books, you'll know that I love models, so in this book, I'll be sharing with you a model called the Recognition Pyramid. I started using it when I was an HR Leader at Reward Gateway, and have been using it ever since as I help companies in my consulting work. I love this model and I look forward to sharing it with you as it's that perfect blend of being strategic and yet practical.

- **Use the book as a playbook.**
  This book is not a textbook, it is not a reference book, it is a playbook. This means that it has a bias for action, giving you not just theory and data, but practical and actionable strategies, approaches, techniques and tips to help you get things done. Pick and choose those that work best to help you create and drive an appreciation and recognition culture at your company. To help you with this, each chapter ends with a "call to action" section so you can start driving change right away!

- **Be inspired by the plays.**
  Half of this book is jam-packed with case studies, or what I call "plays," as this is indeed a playbook. They are intended to inspire and inform by sharing how other companies build and manage their recognition programs in their own unique and meaningful way. I absolutely loved interviewing these companies, and I'm certain you'll love reading the plays, walking away with tons of ideas and inspiration.

Thank you

Let me end by saying thank you. Thank you for giving me the opportunity to share with you in this book all that I've learned over the last 20+ years as well as what I've learned through my research and interviews for this book, which has been tons! I've already started using these lessons in how I design appreciation and recognition strategies and programs for my clients, and I hope that it helps you in the same way. So let's get started . . .

Chapter 1: Unpacking the basics of recognition

Chapter objectives

> **In this chapter, we'll cover:**
>
> - The difference between appreciation, gratitude and recognition, and why it doesn't matter what we call them, but how we act on them.
>
> - How employee recognition has evolved over the years, helping us to understand where we've come from and where we need to get to.
>
> - How recognition can help our people and our businesses in eight different impactful ways.
>
> - The ripple effects that recognition can have on those that give, receive and see it.
>
> - Five key design decisions you need to consider upfront.

Introduction

In this first chapter, I'll start by unpacking the basics, spending a few moments exploring what appreciation and recognition mean, how it's evolved over the years, why it's important, and end with some high-level decisions to think about as you start to develop or revisit your recognition program. For those of you who have read any of my books or have heard me speak at events, this should not be a surprise, for I always start with the basics for these two reasons:

1. So that we're all on the same page on these important and foundational concepts before we begin.

2. So that when you're asked these questions from business leaders or your workforce, you'll have something that you can easily cut and paste to do so – my gift to you!

Defining key terms

In my book *Build it: The Rebel Playbook for Employee Engagement* we said "The problem with employee engagement isn't what we're calling it. The problem is we're failing to make the necessary fundamental changes to our disengaging workplace practices."

I believe the same is true here, for whether we call it gratitude, appreciation or recognition, they're all ultimately working towards the same goal. At their core, gratitude, appreciation and recognition are all about looking for and seeing the moments that matter by doing something constructive, meaningful and personal to make someone feel valued and appreciated for their contributions. The difference in these terms is more about the cause and effect, or to put it quite simply, gratitude and appreciation are what happens when we recognize people in the right way.

Gratitude happens when we appreciate through recognition.

And because this book focuses on the "how" – how to achieve these feelings of appreciation and gratitude – going forward in this book I will be using the term "recognition" more often than the others.

Appreciation is the aspiration and outcome of recognition when it's done well.

The evolution of employee recognition

Before we move forward, it's important to pause for a moment and explore the evolution of employee recognition to understand where we have come from and where we are trying to go. As you've either experienced yourself or will see below, it has evolved significantly over the years as we've come to understand what I like to call its" superpowers." And like any other form of evolution and any other superpower, it means that it's gotten stronger and more effective as we've learned our lessons and as we've harnessed its power.

Here's my personal summary of the "**Four Phases of Employee Recognition**," based on what I've personally been through or seen in my career.

1. The **Thank You for Your Time** Phase
   This first phase is where employee recognition began and is where it's used as a way to thank employees for their years of service.

   It's changed over time, with companies recognizing years of service sooner, and by getting better at selecting recognition gifts that are more meaningful to their employees. It still does, however, focus on recognizing service and not contributions, and only recognizes a small percentage of your overall workforce.

2. The **Best of the Best** Phase
   In this next phase, we came to realize that we needed to thank our employees not only for their years of service but for the contributions they've made to the organization. I call it the "Best of the Best" phase, because this kind of recognition focuses on the top performers, recognizing them at certain times of the year for achieving these accolades.

   It's changed over time by shortening the period of time that recognition happens and also in who nominates and selects the winners. It still does, however, create and drive a culture of winners and losers and, like the previous phase, only recognizes a small percentage of your overall workforce.

3. The **Everyone's Invited to the Party** Phase
   In this next phase, we learned even more about recognition, understanding how it meets our basic human needs – a sense of belonging, feelings of accomplishment and feeling fulfilled – and, as the title says, we started inviting everyone to the recognition party.

We expanded our recognition programs to deliver a feeling of appreciation and gratitude to our entire workforce, changing over time to let everyone recognize one another, and making it more frequent, moving to what is often called "anytime" recognition. This new phase drives a culture of recognition, however, it may not do so in a way that drives and supports a company's strategies and objectives.

4. The **Strategic Recognition** Phase
In this last phase, companies have moved to use recognition as a strategic business tool by showing appreciation and acknowledgment for contributions to the business that link specifically to the company's purpose, mission and values. By doing this, behaviors and efforts are focused on what will help the company succeed, and at the same time, help employees feel appreciated for their ongoing and meaningful contributions.

More recently companies like LinkedIn (see play in Chapter 5) have taken it to that next level by bringing into their recognition program other business and people strategies such as those relating to diversity, inclusion and belonging. This phase, like the last one, drives a culture of recognition and invites everyone to the recognition party. The key difference here is that by basing recognition on strategy, companies are reaping more tangible benefits through recognition.

The importance of employee recognition

The next topic I'd like to unpack answers the question "why is recognition important?," and where I'll be exploring the many ways that it impacts our people and our businesses. And for those of you who, like me, love data and statistics, this section is going to put a huge smile on your face as it includes tons of statistics to help you if and when you need it to build a business case throughout your recognition journey.

One thing I'd like to point out, which is probably obvious but needs to be said, is that all of the benefits I've listed below will only be realized when recognition is done "right" – but more on how to do this in the next chapters. For now, let's explore nine ways that recognition can positively impact our employees and our company, and all of the lovely statistics that go along with them.

1. Recognition **increases employee engagement.**
   Let's start with employee engagement, something that most companies focus on and measure as they've come to see the power it can have on their business. Studies show the positive influence that high employee engagement can have on company sales, revenue, customer service, safety and turnover to name a few, showing the true extent of its impact.

   Recognition has been proven to be a key driver of employee engagement, with an article by Deloitte saying that **employee engagement was 14% higher** in organizations where they practice employee recognition than in those without recognition. This should come as no surprise, for a key driver for engagement is to feel valued, which is a direct result of recognition.

   > **I love this story from my former Gap colleague Eric Severson, who is now the Chief People & Belonging Officer at Neiman Marcus Group. He says,**
   >
   > "When I was at Gap, each year we'd bring together all of our store managers who had the highest quarterly employee engagement scores. When they shared their stories of how they achieved this, one common denominator was that they were masters of appreciation. They had figured out that through creating an environment of appreciation, it would drive employee engagement, which made their people and their store successful."

2. Recognition **fosters a sense of belonging**.
   It's been proven that one of the biggest contributors to employee engagement is a sense of belonging, something can only happen when there is a shared sense of purpose, feeling fully accepted, and where employees genuinely care about one another and have a willingness to invest emotional energy for the benefit of each other. Recognition can be a key contributor to this sense of belonging, with each recognition

act showing the recipient that they're accepted, cared about for who they are and what they've done, and worthy of their recognition efforts.

A study by Glint[10] goes on to show that employees with a strong sense of belonging are over **six times more likely to be engaged** than those who don't, and **12% happier.** And another study by BetterUp found that if employees feel like they belong, companies reap substantial bottom-line benefits such as a **56% increase in job performance**, a **50% drop in turnover**, and a **75% reduction in sick days**. And to bring this to life, the report shows that for a 10,000-person company, this would result in annual savings of more than $52 million.

3. Recognition **increases employee happiness.**
   Employee happiness, like employee engagement, can also have a positive impact on a business. In Shawn Archer's book *The Happiness Advantage,* he talks about how happiness leads to employees who feel more positive, are more creative, are better at solving problems, and are more effective collaborators, all of which contribute to a more successful company.

   And what is that connection to recognition? Well, according to a study by The Boston Consulting Group[11] that ranked the 26 factors of happiness on the job, they found that "the most important single job element for all people is appreciation for their work," which, as we know, occurs through recognition.

   The reason for this is partly down to fulfilling basic human needs, but also down to science, as "happiness chemicals," which are dopamine, serotonin, oxytocin and endorphin, are released when you are recognized. This means that by recognizing someone you are giving them the gift of happiness.

---

10   2020 Insights Report by Glint.
11   2014 study done by Boston Consulting Group.

4. Recognition **supports employee wellbeing**.
    Related to happiness, and something new that I added to
    my list during the COVID-19 pandemic, is the impact that
    recognition can have on wellbeing. We've seen that in a world
    filled with uncertainty and challenges, recognition was used
    as a way to give hope and strength to our workforces, lifting
    their spirits and helping them be more resilient. As businesses
    and their workforces continue to face everyday challenges,
    recognition can and will be a way to support overall wellbeing
    objectives.

    An example of a company that used recognition in this way
    throughout the pandemic is EDF Energy, which sent the
    following three mailings to each and every employee during
    the lockdown period to make them feel appreciated:

    •   The first mailing was sent out at the beginning of
        lockdown, and included a tea bag, a cookie and a note that
        said "We're really grateful for everything you do, and think
        you're one smart cookie."

    •   Another mailing was sent in July and included a bag
        of candy and a note that said "If we could choose our
        colleagues we'd definitely pick you. Thank you for your
        hard work."

    •   And finally, employees received a "Little Box of
        Appreciation," containing two recognition cookies and 50
        recognition notes. The notes were of inspiration, gratitude
        and motivation, and came with instructions to open when
        needed.

A little recognition can provide a morale boost

To better understand the effectiveness of symbolic recognition for public sector employees, a study[12] was run to look at the impact of sending social workers personalized letters of appreciation to their home addresses. They randomly assigned half of the social workers to receive letters from their direct managers, while the other half did not receive a letter.

The letters contained two sentences of positive feedback. The first sentence was selected from a menu of options such as, "your work has consistently had a positive impact on the children you work with," and "your continued dedication and hard work make children and families in the region better off every day," and the second sentence was written by the manager themselves. In this way, they ensured that the letters were reasonably standardized but still personalized.

One month after this simple intervention, the social workers who received a letter **reported feeling significantly more valued, more recognized for their work, and more supported by their organization** than those who didn't receive a letter. There were also positive (though not quite statistically significant) impacts on subjective wellbeing, belonging, intrinsic motivation, and sickness absence rates for social workers who received letters.

5. Recognition **increases employee trust.**
   Employee trust is another factor that has been proven to have a positive impact on the success of a company. From productivity to innovation, companies with high levels of trust have been found to outperform those with low levels of trust.

   And again, recognition has an important part to play, with a study[13] by Workhuman saying that one of the most effective ways of building trust for managers and senior leaders is through frequent recognition. They found that employees who were recognized were **34% more likely to trust senior leaders** and **33% more likely to trust managers**, compared to those who had never been recognized.

---

12 Research conducted by Shibeal O'Flaherty, Michael T. Sanders and Ashley Whillans, and shared in an article in the Harvard Business Review in March 2021.
13 2016 WorkHuman Research Institute report

Adding to this, according to a study by Gallup, 66% of those who said they received team-based recognition agreed with this statement: "I trust the colleagues with whom I work on a regular basis," compared to only 26% who said they don't receive team-based recognition.

6. Recognition **increases employee awareness.**
   This next way moves from how the employee *feels* as a result of being recognized, to *what they receive:* An increased sense of awareness. This happens through feedback, which is formally and informally given each and every time an employee is recognized. It lets them know which of their efforts are most appreciated and valued, and gives them a sense of achievement, and an awareness of which actions and behaviors they should continue to focus on to lead to greater success. It also adds additional levels to feedback, moving it from linear – good or bad – to cover more bases and more situations.

   Feedback through recognition quiets the negative voices that take up so much of our thoughts and time, helping us know that we're on the right track, that what we do matters and is truly making a difference.

   According to a paper[14] by Gallup, "Recognition helps individuals accurately assess their performance. It provides the data we need to master new tasks and demands. It creates positive emotions, inspires broader perspectives and stimulates creative thinking — all at the foundation of innovation."

7. Recognition **increases employee productivity.**
   As shown in the previous data, it's not just employees who benefit from recognition, the company does as well. One way is through an increase in productivity, since having employees who are engaged, happy, trusting, aware and connected naturally leads to a more productive work environment. Recognition is a simple way to highlight what good and great

---

14 2016 article by Gallup titled "Employee Recognition: Low Cost, High Impact"

look like in a business, leading to improved productivity as more and more employees mirror these behaviors.

A study by Reward Gateway shows that **79% of employees would work harder** if they felt their efforts were being recognized, and research done by Shawn Achor shows that **employee productivity can increase by 30%** when employees receive just one piece of praise a day.

And it's not just the receiver of recognition that is more productive. According to research by Shawn Achor, people who provide "social support" (which includes praising the actions of others) were 10 times more likely to be productive than peers who didn't praise as often. As an added bonus, they were also more likely to be promoted.

8. Recognition **drives business results**.
   Next, and something that should not be a surprise, is that these impacts will ultimately help your company be more successful and achieve higher business results.

   According to a study by Josh Bersin, companies that excel at employee recognition on average are **12 times more likely to generate strong business results** than their peers. And to make it even more compelling, according to the Gallup State of the American Workplace report, if organizations would double the number of employees who receive recognition for their work on a weekly basis, they would experience a **24% improvement in quality** and a **10% reduction in shrinkage**, both which contribute to strong business results.

9. Recognition **reduces employee turnover.**
   And finally, recognition can have an impact on employee turnover, with employees staying longer because they feel valued and appreciated through recognition. We often believe that pay is the number one reason people leave a company, but in fact, a study by Reward Gateway found that **79% of employees who quit their job cited a lack of recognition as the key driver**.

And for those who have not left their company, a study[15] by Gallup found that employees who do not feel adequately recognized are **twice as likely to say they'll quit in the next year.**

People respond to praise, even from a robot

A study was conducted at a New York state hospital to increase the frequency by which hospital employees washed their hands as this was deemed extremely important for preventing the spread of disease. After warning signs and live video monitors were placed by hand sanitizer stations, only 10% of hospital employees were washing their hands. However, when an electronic board was placed in the hallway of the unit that gave employees instant feedback when they washed their hands, displaying a positive message such as "Good job!", the rate of compliance rose to 90% within four weeks. The study shows the power of our need to be praised for good behavior, even when it's from an electronic robot!

The ripple effects of recognition

Another impact of recognition is something called the "ripple effect," which happens when employees receive, give and even see recognition being given to colleagues. In psychology, they call this the "emotional contagion in groups," which talks about how moods, emotions and actions are transferred within groups.

> **"The more you help people find their light, the brighter you both will shine."**
> *Big Potential* – **Shawn Achor**

Here are three ways this ripple effect happens through recognition:

1. The first has to do with giving more recognition after receiving it yourself. According to a study, employees who are recognized are **three times more likely to recognize someone else**, calling this "positive reciprocity," and creating a ripple or domino effect as more people are recognized,

---

15 2016 article by Gallup titled "Employee Recognition: Low Cost, High Impact"

which turns into more people recognizing others, and so on and so on.

2. The next can be seen in companies where recognition is shared and celebrated socially through technology. In these scenarios, there are two effects as a consequence of employees viewing the recognition messages. First, they can join in on the recognition by adding their own message and rippling and multiplying the effect it has on the receiver. Second, they can be inspired by the recognition to send out their own recognition message, rippling and multiplying the number of people receiving recognition.

3. And finally, there's an effect that I call "memory moments," which happens when we create memory moments through recognition that we experience when we receive it and also when we think back to it for years to come. I personally have many of these stored away in my mind and even my desk drawer, pulling them out every once in a while when I need a bit of a pick-me-up or a reminder of the value and impact that I've made.

NAHL Group plc (see play in Chapter 5) created an additional recognition "ripple effect" by starting a practice of recognizing the recognizer. The way it works is that from time to time the person receiving the recognition sends a "hug" to the person who recognized them to show them that they are appreciated for their recognition actions and the difference they're making. It's a nice touch that creates new recognition moments and more ripples.

Key design decisions

The last area I'd like to unpack is the high-level design decisions that you'll need to make as you design or redesign your recognition programs. I thought it would be helpful to share these now so that you can start to become familiar with them before we get into the building phase. Please note that in the following chapters I'll be sharing tips and strategies to help you make these key decisions, so don't worry if you can't yet make them.

Five Key Design Decisions

1. What are we trying to achieve through recognition?

Here is where you decide **why** your company and your people need recognition. As shown in the previous section, there are lots of ways that recognition can make an impact, but the key here is making sure that in the short and long term you focus on those that are most important to your people and your company.

2. Who will give and receive the recognition?

Next, you'll want to decide **who** in your organization will be able to give and receive recognition. Is it only your managers or is it your entire workforce? Is it all countries, departments or job levels, or specific ones based on specific needs?

3. What will employees receive when recognized?

Your next step is to decide **what** employees will receive when they are recognized. Will it be non-financial, financial or a combination? Although this may seem like a straightforward question to answer, much of the magic in recognition is in getting this right.

4. When will employees be recognized?

Up next is choosing **when** your employees will be recognized, looking at the frequency of the different elements of your recognition program. As with the other questions, the answer needs to link directly back to your "why," delivering recognition at the right time to meet your recognition objectives.

5. How will you manage your recognition program?

Lastly, you'll need to determine **how** you'll manage your recognition program. Will it be paper-based, through a recognition technology platform, or a combination? Getting this right (or wrong) can be the difference between you succeeding (or failing!) through recognition.

Calls to Action:

Think about which of the four phases your company's employee recognition program is in now, and where you want and need it to be in the future.

Now:

In the Future:

Review the list of the nine ways that recognition can make an impact, and rank them from high to low as to which are the most critical at your company to deliver on your purpose, mission and business objectives.

1.

2.

3.

4.

5.

6.

7.

8.

Chapter 2: The golden rules of recognition

Chapter objectives

> **In this chapter, we'll cover:**
>
> - Why and how it's important to recognize in a meaningful way, both in what you say and what you do, while understanding and respecting the diverse needs of your workforce.
>
> - Why and how it's important to recognize in a unified and inclusive way, looking at how recognition can be given, received and used.
>
> - Why and how it's important to put recognition under the spotlight, maximizing and multiplying its power.
>
> - Why and how it's important to recognize frequently in a timely way, leaning into "in the moment" recognition to shorten the gap between achievements and recognition moments to meet your recognition objectives.

Introduction

The purpose of this chapter is to share with you some guiding principles to help the design or redesign of your recognition program. I call these the "golden rules" of recognition as they align with the ideology of golden rules, which focus on kindness and thoughtfulness, which can help us all in our quest to deliver appreciation through recognition.

Though they might seem theoretical at first, I believe that they are practical and actionable and will guide you to new ways of driving strategic and meaningful change at your organization. I've been using these for years now myself, and they've helped keep me on track while also challenging my traditional thinking.

To help you remember the rules, I'd like to introduce you to an acronym – **MUST**. The acronym came about five years ago when I was doing a presentation on the topic of recognition at a conference, and I wanted to find a way to help my audience understand the things they must do to get their recognition program right. I ended up with this word as it not only creates a call to action, we "must" do this, but each letter neatly sums up key points to help us deliver on our recognition objectives.

M	U	S	T
Make it **M**eaningful	Make it **U**nified	Shine a **S**potlight on it	Make it **T**imely

I've evolved my explanation as the world and as my thoughts on recognition have changed since that first presentation, but since my audiences and clients around the world continue to find it helpful, I'd like to share it with you. Here we go:

M – Make recognition meaningful

Let's start with the letter "M," which stands for making employee recognition **meaningful**. This is critical so that the recipient truly feels recognized, and it happens when you deliver meaning in both what **you say** and **what you do**, showing the person that you have seen, value and appreciate their specific contributions. And as you'll see as you read this section, it's not just one simple step to take to achieve this, but a variety of actions that are, you guessed it, *meaningful*.

Can you ever give too much recognition?

At a conference recently I shared a story about a company where 94% of their employees had been recognized, saying what a great achievement this was. Afterward, I was asked the question, "Can you ever give too much recognition, does it get watered down if it's given too often?"

My response was yes and no. Yes, because if the recognition is not given in a meaningful way then yes, it can take away from and water down genuine recognition. And no, because as long as recognition is given in a meaningful way, then it is never too much. For example, if someone does something worth recognizing at 9:00 am and then does something different that is worth recognizing at 10:00 am, recognize them both!

Getting recognition messages right

The "say," which are your recognition messages, is absolutely critical to the success of a recognition moment. Saying "thanks for your help," although very nice, does little to make the person feel recognized since there's likely little to no understanding of what they've done to merit that recognition. If instead, the message says, "Thanks for coming in early to prepare and distribute materials to the team to help them understand how the new office scheduling system will work," the person knows specifically what they've done, and how they've helped you and others.

> **By creating meaningful recognition messages, you multiply the impact of the appreciation, taking it to an entirely new level.**

> **"Gratitude is not just a matter of showering more 'thank-yous' and 'we think you're greats' on employees. Hardly. It is not a rote checklist item or perfunctorily high-fiving team members. For expressions of gratitude to work their magic, they must be genuine and specific."**
> *Leading with Gratitude* – **Adrian Gostick and Chester Elton**

Since writing these messages does not come naturally for most people, it's important to educate and train your employees on the "art" of creating meaningful recognition messages. Let me share with you the approach I use in my training, which is from Gregg Lederman's book *Crave*, and follows these three steps using the "AVI" approach:

Step 1: A	Step 2: V	Step 3: I
Tell the **Action**	Connect to a **Value**	Share the **Impact**

1. Tell the **Action**: Describe what the person did, their behavior or action, that is worthy of being recognized.
   Example: Thank you, Chloe, for taking the time out of your busy schedule to review and edit my draft book.

2. Connect to a **Value:** Next, link the behavior or action to your company values or specific company objectives. By doing this, it makes it clear that what the person did makes a difference in achieving a priority or goal for the organization, with no second-guessing.
   Example: Chloe, your actions directly align with my company value of "create magic" and my objective of creating a book that is useful and engaging for my readers.

3. Share the **Impact**: Last, but certainly not least, it's important to show the benefit and impact of the behavior or action that you are recognizing. As Lederman says, "By sharing the impact, you are providing another healthy dose of respect and purpose!"
   Example: Chloe, your edits had such a profound impact on the final version of the book, with it being at least 10 times better than it ever would have been without your help. Thank you, you rock!

Pitfalls to avoid

These three "AVI" steps are fantastic, and I've seen them make a huge difference in helping my employees understand how to craft meaningful messages. However, if we don't avoid certain pitfalls and situations, then it doesn't matter how lovely the message is, it will still fall flat on its face. Here are three of the most common pitfalls I've encountered, which I suggest you highlight when you communicate and train others on the art of meaningful recognition:

1. **Hollow praise**: The first pitfall is "hollow praise," which is defined as "lacking real substance, value, or meaning; insincere or false." I describe it as the "eye-rolling praise," – you know the kind, where someone reads it out in a meeting and everyone rolls their eyes because they believe it to be so untrue. For these, "silence is golden" as the expression goes, as it's better to say nothing than to give hollow praise.

2. **Comparison praise**: The next pitfall is what Shawn Achor calls "comparison-based praise," where phrases such as "the best," "the smartest," and "the funniest" are used.

   "We have been taught that we live in a survival of the fittest world, so we praise the wrong way — using comparison-based praise, we lift up one by diminishing another, creating a hierarchy," Achor said in an interview.[16] In addition, he says that it "subconsciously limits the recipient by framing their success as a new standard of achievement — and pressures that person to continue meeting the same level of success in each future endeavor."

   Achor recommends avoiding comparison-based praise, instead giving authentic feedback, focusing specifically on what the person did well during a certain activity.

3. **"Piss off" praise**: The final pitfall is something I refer to as the "piss off" factor, and the best way to describe it is with a story. The situation was that six colleagues and I received the same group message to thank us for our contributions in delivering a presentation at a conference. The message was written following the three steps shared previously, which is great, but since we all contributed differently (e.g. one person had spent months researching the topic, another a week preparing the graphics, and another spending only 15 minutes

16   Shared in Thrive Global article titled "We're Actually Praising People the Wrong Way — Here's Why"

giving attendees handouts as they entered the room), the result was some pissed off people as some of us felt that the thanks was hollow and not personal enough.

In these situations, it's important to take the time to recognize individuals for their individual contributions. If everyone in the group had the same action, behavior and impact, then maybe you can send a group message, but before you do this, ask yourself "will I piss anyone off by doing this?"

Creating meaning in what you recognize

Just as important as the "say" is the "do," which I'd like to look at in two ways – what do we do to create meaning *for the employee* in how we recognize them, and how do we create meaning *for the company* by recognizing the "right" things?

Getting recognition awards right

Let's start by looking at it from the employees' perspective. I'll be going into lots of detail in the next chapter on how to determine your recognition awards, both non-financial and financial, so for now let me make the point that it is critical to take the time to get this right. Don't just throw money, gifts or anything else at your employees as a way to award recognition efforts without care and thought attached to it. Forgetting the "Say" means you'll end up with that cringe-worthy disconnect, and completely negate the positives derived from recognition.

For example, I was once asked to approve a recognition award in the amount of $1,000 for a member of my five-person global rewards team. When I asked the nominator why they wanted to give this, they explained it was because the employee had done such a great job helping with his group's annual pay review process. The issue I had with this was that it created a disconnect between the say and the do, in that it was too large of a reward for essentially what is a part of that person's job. By rewarding in this way, it could have had both short and long-term impacts.

Going back to pissing people off, the other four members of my team would have been very pissed off as they had worked just as hard and did not receive such a reward. How did the story end? Well, I thanked the nominator for his kind gesture, explained my concerns, and suggested that he send a meaningful and heartfelt handwritten card to thank the employee personally for their contributions. He did just that, the employee was over the moon receiving the card, and the say and do remained intact.

Values-based recognition

It's equally important to make sure that you create meaning in how you "do" recognition by recognizing those actions and behaviors that don't just help your employees feel appreciated but help your business achieve their objectives and success. If you don't do this, then quite frankly you're flushing the time and money you spend on recognition down the drain.

The most effective way to do this is by recognizing your employees against your company values. As I talk about in my book *Bringing Your Values Out to Play*, this does three things:

1. You **create focus**, like a dartboard, showing your employees the target they are shooting for.

2. You **signal that values are important** – putting them front and center and not hidden away in an employee handbook or on a poster hanging in the office.

3. You create **habits** by recognizing against those values, creating a feedback loop as the values and the meaning behind them become second nature to your employees.

Recognizing your people against your company values is like a live classroom experience, teaching and demonstrating what your values mean and how they look in real-time, and in the moment.

And the good news is that this translates into positives for your company as well. According to a study by SHRM[17], companies with values-based recognition programs reap these benefits:

- They are two times more likely to reinforce and drive business results.

- They are four times more likely to have their employees say that they believe in their company values.

The other good news is that it doesn't need to be difficult to incorporate your values into your recognition program. If you use e-cards, which are as the name suggests, digital recognition cards, you can create a set of values-based e-cards, if you don't, you could create a set of values postcards or create values-based emojis to use on your online communications tool.

Understanding and respecting differences

To end this section, I want to spend a moment addressing the importance of understanding and respecting individual differences when it comes to recognition, making it an integral part of how you live out your DEI (diversity, equity and inclusion) strategy. Going back to making recognition meaningful, this is important so that recognition is viewed as meaningful to **all** members of your diverse workforce.

One difference is based on our **generation**, which comes from different perspectives and experiences. According to a study by the Incentive Research Foundation[18] (IRF), different generations prefer recognition in different ways.

---

17 2018 study done by SHRM.
18 2015 study done by the Incentive Research Foundation.

Let me share with you some of the differences that I've seen over the years in how you should recognize people from different generations, but do keep in mind that few people fall neatly into these definitions. By all means, use this as a reference point, but more importantly, take the time to truly understand your people before making judgments or jumping to conclusions.

- **Baby Boomers:** This group grew up in a world where recognition was rarely spoken about and rarely given. If it was, it was given as a thank you for their years with the company, or for contributions on specific work or projects through ad hoc or annual bonuses. It was very much top-down, so recognition was given from the company, possibly from their manager.

  What this means is that recognition, especially recognition given regularly, may not be something that is expected or natural to them as it wasn't part of their upbringing. You'll need to help them understand the power of recognition, making them feel comfortable giving and receiving it. They may, however, expect to be recognized for years of service, since this was the norm for them. Keep this in mind if you decide to remove or change your long service program, as it may be seen as something very important to them.

- **Generation X:** This group grew up in a world where more regular recognition was slowly becoming common practice with the introduction of programs such as annual recognition awards or possibly quarterly awards. It was again top-down, with it coming from the company but also more and more from their manager.

  What this means is that recognition is something that they are more familiar with, but since it was only given to the "best of the best," it may not be something they expect. They may not be comfortable with giving recognition, thinking that recognition needs to be rationed for only the best, and also because they may not have experience with the concept of peer-to-peer recognition. You'll need to help them understand that recognition is a gift that can, and should, be given often, recognizing behaviors and actions "in the moment," so recognizing everyday moments that have an impact on their colleagues and the business.

- **Generation Y**: Generation Y, often called the "trophy generation" when it comes to recognition, grew up receiving a trophy for everything and anything in their personal life, and at work, many would have had been exposed to a continuous approach to recognition, where it's given more frequently. They would have also experienced recognition from many directions, so not just top-down from the company and their managers

  What this means is they expect recognition to be less formal and more frequent, not wanting to wait five years for a long service award or a year for an annual award. They expect recognition to mirror how they recognize and react to their friends outside of work, which is in a social context.

- **Generation Z:** This group has grown up in a world where technology is all around them, using and relying on it to help them as they go about their day. Integral to this is the use of social media, using it as a way to connect and interact with their friends and the world around them.

  What this means is that they expect recognition to behave similarly, being able to access and be a part of recognition as easily and as often as they do with Snapchat, Instagram, or whatever social media platform they use. Even more so than Generation Y, they will have little interest and patience for any program that involves too much effort or does not allow the social side of it.

Another difference is based on our **personality**. In a blog written by Alexandra Powell, Director of Client Culture and Engagement at Reward Gateway, she talks about the importance of "making sure to understand others' preferences to prevent misunderstandings and ensure your appreciation is well received on the other end!"

In Alex's blog, she uses the Insights Personality Assessment model to break down how each of the four personality colors like to receive recognition. I found this so helpful that I wanted to share it with you below. As I said with generational differences, do use this as one of many tools to help you understand these differences.

- **Blue:** They are naturally very precise or deliberate, so you may be met with resistance rather than appreciation when you recognize them. You may hear, "But the project isn't yet done – let's wait to see how it turns out before we celebrate." or "I was just doing my job and I made some mistakes."

  Remind this person to celebrate the "small wins," and remember that they may not be comfortable with grandiose public displays of appreciation. They are less likely to appear excited by the praise, but this doesn't mean they haven't heard it. Focus on the facts of how their work is impacting others to make it more likely they will hear the recognition

- **Yellow:** They are enthusiastic and sociable, so they're more likely to be looking for consistent, positive feedback, with it fueling and motivating their performance. If you do have constructive feedback for them, you will be more successful if you start with the positive so they feel "seen."

  Others of different styles may see this behavior as shallow or ego-driven, but when enthusiastic or sociable people get consistent recognition, their positive energy can support the whole team to be better.

- **Red:** They are determined and competitive, find receiving recognition natural, but won't want to spend too much time delving into the recognition. They may benefit from taking time to think through not just the win, but how they helped contribute to the win.

  They may seem to get impatient with too much debrief after a result. Don't feel offended if they don't open up or seem grateful for the recognition on the surface, but feel reassured that deep down it means a lot to them.

- **Green:** They are encouraging and patient, and will want to feel that the recognition they're receiving is genuine. As with all the others, taking time to share what they did and why it was important – especially how it fulfills the higher purpose or values of the organization – will be very well received

  This group is the most likely to thank you for thanking them but then may try to deflect the praise unto others in the group that contributed to the success.

These are just two ways to look at diversity, but as you know, there are many more that need to be taken into consideration such as nationality, culture, gender, language to name a few. The key here is to **pause and take the time to fully understand and respect differences and then use them to deliver the most meaningful recognition to that individual.**

U – Make recognition unified

The next golden rule follows on from what was mentioned most recently about diversity and focuses on designing recognition programs that are unified and inclusive. It's important that recognition does not create a divide or wedge between your workforce, with the "haves" and "have nots" based on location, department, manager or function, to name a few.

Instead, recognition needs to be universal, making it available for all to give and all to receive, thus increasing your chances of creating a recognition culture and achieving your recognition objectives.

This is so important that I was thinking of changing the letter from "U" to "I" in my acronym to drive the focus on inclusion. However, I think you'll agree that MIST doesn't have the same impact as MUST, so I'll keep it as is, but make sure to create the alignment between these two words.

In Frances Frei and Anne Morriss's book *Unleashed*, they share an "Inclusion Dial," which lists four elements that they believe create a culture of inclusion:

Safe – Employees feel physically and emotionally safe in the workplace, regardless of who they are.

Welcome – Employees feel welcome in the workplace, regardless of who they are; they can bring their "whole selves" to work without penalty.

Celebrated – Employees feel celebrated in the workplace because of who they are; they are rewarded for contributing their unique ideas and perspectives.

Cherished – A culture of inclusion permeates the organization; leaders embrace differences among employees as a source of competitive advantage, and there is minimal variability in the experience of belonging across individuals, teams, and functions.

This shows, directly and indirectly, the importance of recognition in creating a culture of inclusion.

A unified approach to giving recognition

The first part of being unified and inclusive has to do with who you allow to **give recognition** through the design of your programs. When companies limit it to just managers a few things can happen. First, it creates a "them" and "us" situation as employees miss out on the opportunity of giving recognition, which has been proven to be just as important as receiving recognition. And second, it limits the number of recognition moments that are given as it reduces the number of people involved, which can directly or indirectly lead to feelings of exclusion.

For this reason, more and more companies have adopted a peer-to-peer approach to recognition, or what I like to think of as a "crowdsourcing" approach to recognition, as it encourages your people to work together to create and have collective responsibility for recognition. By working together, all of the positive impacts of recognition shared in the last chapter are multiplied, with more eyes, ears and hearts looking for and capturing recognition moments.

**Peer-to-peer recognition crowdsources recognition
– having more eyes, ears and hearts looking
for and capturing recognition moments.**

Here are three ways that peer-to-peer recognition can have a positive impact:

1. **Financial results** – According to a study by SHRM[19], peer-to-peer recognition is **36% more likely to have a positive impact on financial results** over manager-only recognition.

2. **Performance** – According to a study by Gartner[20] that looked at performance, they found that feedback shared through peer-to-peer recognition can **enhance performance by as much as 14%**.

    "As work becomes more interdependent and managers have less direct visibility into the day-to-day of their teams, high-quality peer input has become an essential part of effective performance feedback," says Jessica Knight, research director at Gartner, in the study.

3. **Team culture** – According to a study by O.C. Tanner[21], peer-to-peer recognition **increases the probability of a constructive team culture by 2.5 times**. It goes on to say that it also strengthens the connections between employees and increases their psychological safety.

---

19 SHRM/Globoforce 2012 Employee Recognition Survey.
20 Gartner research 2018.
21 O.C. Tanner's 2020 Global Culture Report.

Being "positive nodes" to one another

In Shawn Achor's book *Big Potential*, he defines small potential as the "limited success you can achieve alone" and big potential as the "success you can achieve only in a virtuous cycle with others."

He explains that by becoming a "positive node" in your workplace, and helping those around you "improve their creativity, their productivity, their abilities, their performance, and more, you are not only helping the group become better; you are exponentially increasing your own potential for success."

This is exactly what peer-to-peer recognition does, allowing us all to be positive nodes, or what I like to think of as one another's "**success cheerleaders**"!

At Atlassian (see play in Chapter 5), all of their recognition programs are based on the principles of peer-to-peer recognition, from Kudos to Big Kudos, they all allow employees to give different forms of recognition.

"Recognizing your peers is huge. The value we create for our customers occurs from working across boundaries, functions, time zones, borders, and customs. And when we live our value of "play as a team" across Atlassian to benefit our customers, we should celebrate and recognize that behavior. By doing this, it's created a brilliant network effect of how we work across teams and functions, to work more effectively together. It's about pulling together," says Dominic Price, Work Futurist at Atlassian.

Let me end this part by saying that although I am a huge fan of peer-to-peer recognition, depending on your culture, values and overall objectives of your recognition program, there may be reasons for allowing only managers to give recognition under a specific plan or program. For example, at a previous company, I put in place something called the "Leadership Amazing" awards. The goal of these was to highlight truly amazing work, and because it was so amazing, we felt that the recognition should come from a member of our leadership team to have a greater impact. While the leaders received inputs from others in the business, we wanted the impact of the recognition moment to be greater, and having it directly come from a leader made the recognition moment feel "bigger" than our other recognition tactics.

A unified approach to receiving recognition

The next part of making recognition unified and inclusive has to do with who can **receive recognition**, and I believe this is an area where much work still needs to be done. Too often, we put limits on who can be recognized, e.g. only one person can win employee of the month, or only six people can win employee of the year, etc. Here are some of the negative things that can happen when we do this:

1. **Feelings of exclusion** – Limiting the number of people who can be recognized often leads to others feeling excluded, creating what I mentioned earlier with the "haves" and "have nots." This goes against the grain of a unified and inclusive approach to recognition, putting up barriers and closing the door on recognition for many of your hard-working employees.

2. **Negative reactions** – It can also lead to negative reactions from those not winning the recognition awards, or as I call them, the "eye-rollers." This happens when the names are called out and people roll their eyes and say things to themselves or to others like, "what did they do to win, I did the exact same thing as them," or "I can't believe they won again, they're such a favorite," or even "I give up, why work so hard if I'm never recognized!"

3. **Creates more losers than winners** – Next, this can lead to your employees feeling like either a winner or a loser, with the few, your top 5-10% of employees feeling like winners and the remaining 90-95% of employees feeling like losers.

4. **Leaves out your "glue people"** – Limiting recognitions can also leave out what Eric Hutcherson, Chief People & Inclusion Officer at Universal Group, calls his "glue people." He explained that when he was at the National Basketball Association they had their stars and their glue people, who were those that held the team together. He went on to say that if we only recognized our stars, or in basketball terms, our scorers, we were completely ignoring those that make the assists or grab the rebounds or play great defense. These

people, your glue people, are the ones that day after day show up and contribute to the success of your company, and if you don't recognize them will walk away and leave your star players standing alone on the "court."

5. **Reduces the power of recognition** – Finally, with fewer people being recognized it will naturally lead to fewer recognition moments which will directly impact the overall power and benefits of recognition. It's simple math!

We need to practice "equal opportunity" recognition, looking at recognition through an inclusion lens, making sure that everyone has an equal opportunity to be noticed, appreciated and recognized.

> At Neiman Marcus Group they have a recognition program called "NMG Best," which recognizes the best of the best teams and individuals from across the organization. It's done in a unified and inclusive manner in that everyone gets to nominate and vote on winners, and they celebrate the achievements together as a community.
>
> "More and more, the awards are recognizing teams versus individuals, emphasizing the increasingly cross-functional collaboration and teamwork required to achieve results in an interconnected, global, and digital world. This public recognition of team achievements reinforces our strategic objective of increasing collaboration across the enterprise to drive speed, innovation, and enhanced customer experience," says Eric Severson, Chief People & Belonging Officer at Neiman Marcus.

The *MasterChef* approach to winners and losers

So what can we do to recognize those that truly and genuinely excel and contribute at a higher level than others? How can we have winners without making everyone else feel defeated, zapped of their drive and engagement, and feeling like losers? This was a question I racked my brain trying to figure out how best to answer until I was watching *MasterChef Australia*, a show where amateur chefs battle it out week after week to be crowned the champion. And it came to me, yes they only have one winner at the end of the season, but as contestants face elimination tests and one by one leave the show as losers, they actually leave as winners. Here's how I believe they get it right:

- **There are multiple opportunities to be a winner.**
  Throughout the series, there are many opportunities to celebrate contestant successes and to feel like winners, such as making it to the next level or winning individual cooking competitions. In fact, throughout the series, most contestants at one point in time have this winning feeling.

- **There are many ways to be a winner.**
  One reason why there are so many winners throughout the series is that there are multiple ways to win. Whether it's a team challenge, a skills test, an invention test, they don't just compete in one way throughout the series. By doing this, it allows contestants with different skills to have the opportunity to excel and win.
  Recognition tip: Create multiple recognition plans within your overall program so that there are more opportunities to be recognized.

- **They have mini-winners.**
  For each cooking challenge, they don't just call out the name of the one winner but they call out and bring forward the top three winners of the challenge. By doing this, they are creating mini-winners, who feel like they've achieved something for being called forward and for having positive words being said about their dish, celebrating their successes.
  Recognition tip: Celebrate not just recognition award winners, but runner ups and highly commended.

- **There are constant learning moments.**
  Throughout every challenge, contestants are given feedback from the judges, positive and negative, which helps them learn and grow as chefs. One by one as they leave the show they consistently say the same thing, which is to thank the judges for such an amazing learning experience. In the last episode I watched, the contestant said, "I feel confident in my abilities, like I can fly out the door," which sounds like a winner and not a loser to me!

Recognition tip: Teach your employees how to give meaningful recognition so that recognition provides both appreciation and learning moments.

- **They celebrate when they are eliminated.**
  Although no one likes to lose and have to leave the show, they do this with such genuine respect and admiration, focusing on what they have done and not the fact that they have lost. So much so, that the final thing shared about the contestant in an episode is what they've done next to follow their cooking dream, whether that's an apprenticeship, a food blog or even if they've opened up their own line of sauces. This is how they've taken what they've learned to move forward as a winner – and not a loser.

"I believe the world is big enough that everyone can have success, and that you don't have to lose in order for me to win. We can all coexist, and all have an equal opportunity to be recognized." – Eric Hutcherson, Chief People & Inclusion Officer, Universal Music Group

Let me end this part by saying that there may be some situations when you feel it is important to recognize your "best of the best," those who have genuinely stood out as they have contributed and achieved more than others. If you do this, it's important to get the balance right, having other recognition plans in place to offset some of the negatives I've outlined, and also bring in the lessons shared above from *MasterChef.*

A unified approach to using recognition

And finally, for recognition to be unified and inclusive, it needs to have the opportunity to be used in a consistent way. Far too often we put up hurdles or barriers that prevent some of our people from participating and engaging with recognition, which again leads to the "haves" and the "have nots." If recognition is to be fair and inclusive, these barriers must be removed, so that everyone can use recognition in the way in which it was intended.

Some things to consider here are:

- **Systems** – Technology and systems can be a huge advantage to drive recognition, but if not looked at through the lens of inclusion, it can become a barrier. It's important to look at whether all employees have access to the recognition systems you put in place, and if not, consider alternative ways they can take part in recognition. For example, if not all employees have computers, could the system be available on cell phones? Could recognition messages appear on screens in break rooms so employees can view and celebrate these moments?

- **Budgets** – As you develop your recognition budgets, it's important to understand the impact it can have on teams equally feeling recognized. For example, are the budgets of small teams disproportionate to those of large teams, leading to managers of small teams not having enough to fairly recognize their employees? Are recognition awards at a higher level taking up a disproportionate amount of your overall budget so that smaller awards are being ignored? Make sure that budgets don't get in the way of recognition.

- **Understanding** – The next thing to consider is the understanding (or lack of understanding) that your diverse workforce has when it comes to giving, receiving and getting involved with recognition. For example, do certain employees not send or get involved with recognition because they don't understand why it's important and/or how to use the technology? If so, make sure that your training and communication plans work together to overcome this.

- **Managers** – Finally, it's important that your managers don't directly or indirectly cause problems when it comes to employees being treated in a fair and inclusive way. This could happen if some managers choose not to engage with the programs and/or do so in a way that treats their team unfairly. In Chapter 4 I'll be covering more on this, talking about the importance of managers understanding the role they have to play and how to get it right.

S – Shine a spotlight on recognition

Let's next move on to the letter "S," which stands for shining a spotlight on recognition. In the past, recognition was done in a very private way, between the sender and the receiver, but over the years we've come to see the importance of changing this to put it under the spotlight and watch the magic happen.

Why the spotlight is important

Let me start by sharing five reasons why putting a spotlight on recognition is important and how it can help your company:

1. **It helps celebrate recognition moments.**
   First, it's a great way to shout about and celebrate recognition moments. As a former competitive gymnast, I explain it as giving your employees the podium to stand on to celebrate and be recognized for their achievement with all of your friends cheering you on from the stands.

   And, if you're like my 20-year-old daughter, our latest generation entering the workforce, I've learned that to them, being able to showcase to others the recognition that she's received is even more important than the recognition itself.

2. **It multiplies the impact.**
   Another thing that happens when you put recognition under the spotlight is that it multiplies the impact of the initial recognition, or as I like to think of it, it "stirs the love around." To illustrate this, think back to a time when you posted something either professionally or personally on social media and the lovely recognition messages and reactions that followed. With each one, you got a new appreciation boost, with the impact getting bigger and lasting much longer. Because of this, instead of reaping the benefits of recognition for a few minutes, it can jump to hours if not days!

3. **It shows what good looks like.**
   Next, it shows others in your organization what good looks

like, reinforcing behaviors for the recipient as well as others. If the last point said "hey, look at me," this one says "hey, look at this," as it showcases what's valued and appreciated at your company, creating both awareness and focus.

Think of it like a spotlight being used in a theatre production, shining intensely on specific cast members. This does two things, it highlights their performance to help the audience's focus be placed where it needs to be, and it lights up the stage to help the performers know where to safely go and not go throughout the performance.

Putting it yet another way, as Voltaire says: "Appreciation is a wonderful thing: It makes what is excellent in others belong to us as well."

4. **It helps connect your people.**
   It also gives your employees the opportunity to connect with one another in a positive, meaningful and uplifting way both directly and indirectly. This is especially important in this new hybrid world, with the recognition spotlight connecting a remote workforce by helping them understand what one another is up to, what they've achieved, and what they're doing to support one another.

   At the same time, it helps them directly connect with one another by getting involved with the recognition moments. Whether it's adding comments and emojis if you have a social recognition wall, or clapping and shouting out words of encouragement if the spotlight is done in person (or virtually), this involvement creates a meaningful and important connection.

5. **It encourages more frequent and continuous recognition.**
   And finally, in the previous chapter, I spoke about something called a ripple effect, which is when recognition is sent as a result of receiving recognition yourself. There's another kind of ripple effect that occurs when an employee sees a recognition moment through the spotlight, spurring them on to recognize someone by either being reminded of their

company's recognition program or seeing a recognition moment that makes them think of something that someone else has done for them.

This can be a powerful way to multiply the superpowers of your recognition program, having it done in a more frequent and continuous way. And since Gallup says that employee **recognition should occur more frequently, at least once every seven days**, every little bit helps!

How to spotlight recognition

So how do you put recognition under the spotlight? When I first started out, we did this by sharing recognition stories in our newsletters or during face-to-face events. More recently, companies are doing this through technology, using e-cards and social recognition walls as a way for employees to participate and engage with recognition. By doing this, it multiplies the impacts of recognition in more ways than I could ever have imagined, paving the way for entire workforces to get involved and drive a recognition culture.

Social recognition isn't scary, it's powerful!

I remember the first time I heard about using social media within an employee recognition system — making employee recognition public, for every employee to see. I wasn't excited. I was nervous, not knowing what to expect, and what exactly "social recognition" really meant or what it would do.

My first thoughts were, what if someone sends e-cards for things of a confidential nature? For example, what if they send someone in HR an e-card to say "thank you for your help with the pay increase" or "thank you for ordering my new company car" or even "thank you for helping me with the disciplinary"? Also, what would happen if employees use inappropriate language, and I'm forced to become the "Social Media Police," and monitor each and every one?

Was it really worth the risk to do this? In a word: Yes, for since that first fleeting thought, I've come to realize that social media is ingrained in everyday life so much that it seems unnatural not to bring it into the world of recognition. And for the things I feared happening, they rarely if ever, happen.

If you don't use recognition technology yet, don't worry, there are still ways to put the spotlight on your recognition moments. Here are a few to get started that I've taken from the plays in Chapter 5, but keep in mind that the key is to figure out what will work best at your company based on your culture and your ways of working.

- **Share stories at company meetings.**
  Since at Atlassian, it's the story that is important, their recognition stories are shared during the monthly global town hall call, with the sender telling the story and sharing the positive behaviors.

- **Share stories during onboarding.**
  At the University of Lincoln, they take case studies from their annual recognition awards and weave them into their onboarding process to show what good looks like and to highlight how recognition is done.

- **Create digital badges.**
  At Shell Energy Retail, they created digital badges that employees are awarded for receiving three or more recognition nominations for the same company value. These can then be displayed in their email signature, which showcases to their global colleagues over and over again their recognition actions.

Let me end this section with a caution that goes back to the concept of diversity and inclusion. Remember that not everyone likes their recognition to go under the spotlight. So before you do this, make sure that you understand what the recipient is comfortable with and what would negate the impact of recognition because of the negative impact the spotlight could create.

T – Make recognition timely

The last letter of the acronym is "T," which stands for making recognition timely, and focuses on the "when" of recognition. We've made strides in this area, reflecting on what we've learned and how we've responded to changes in the workplace, but there is still much work to be done.

According to one survey[22], only 36% of companies are giving timely recognition, meaning that **employees at six in 10 companies are having to wait to receive recognition**.

The word "timely" means to do something in an appropriate time frame, which is a bit wishy-washy, as what does "appropriate time frame" really mean? I believe that this is part of the problem as we all interpret it differently. Does it mean giving recognition once a week, once a month? What, exactly, is the "appropriate time frame" to give recognition? I propose that instead, we focus the definition and our efforts on the gap, the time frame between the moment the behavior or action happens and the moment the recognition occurs.

> **Why wait until a certain day of the week or month to give recognition, why not give it now before you forget AND the impact of the recognition wears off?**

If we remove the hurdles and make giving recognition easy, there is no excuse for waiting, and we can all move to what is commonly called "in the moment" recognition. Now I know that not everyone is there yet, which is why I'll share tips later in the book on it, but wouldn't it be great to set this as a goal of where you want to get to?

Whenever I do a talk on recognition and want to make the point about timely recognition, I have in my slide deck a photo of my husband and me from our wedding day. I ask the audience a few questions – First, if my husband said he loved me every five, 10, 15 years, do you think I would feel loved and appreciated? Next, if my husband cooked a lovely meal for us for dinner, should he have to wait until the end of the month or quarter to be thanked?

Obviously, the answer to these questions is no. I shouldn't have to wait to be told that I'm appreciated and my husband shouldn't have to wait to be thanked. Timely and continuous recognition is not just important to keep a marriage together, but a work relationship as well!

Frequency matters

Another element of the "when" of recognition relates to the frequency of recognition. We've made improvements here as well, increasing the frequency through redesigning our recognition programs, but there's still work to be done. According to the survey mentioned above, only 25% of companies are giving *frequent* recognition, which they define as recognition given multiple times a month, meaning that **employees at almost eight out of 10 companies are not receiving frequent recognition**.

I believe this happens for two reasons:

1. **Companies are recognizing only big wins.**
   First, this is because recognition programs are designed to recognize only those big wins, or what I've heard called "episodic" events. The problem with this is that you miss all of those small wins along the way along with the opportunity to recognize them, multiplying the power of recognition. As my fortune cookie said just the other day, "Two small jumps are sometimes better than one big leap."

   Another way to look at this is that you are recognizing the outcome and not the process and steps you've taken to get to the win. It would be like training for a marathon and not acknowledging all of the steps and individual goals you've achieved to get you there. A tip shared with me by Ben Davies, a U.K. Fitness Consultant, is to break it down into **"non-scale victories"** (NSV) which are those small but important achievements. For example, that first run, the run you do on a rainy day so that you hit your mile goal for the week, and so on. "If you don't acknowledge and celebrate these NSVs you lose motivation, focus, and often, give up on the goal entirely," says Davies.

2. **Companies and leaders are rationing recognition.**
   Secondly because people are rationing their recognition.
   I've seen it time and time again when managers come to me
   and ask – if I've recognized someone last week, is it OK to
   recognize them again today? My question back to them is –
   have they done something that should be recognized? If the
   answer is yes, then do it, and if the answer is no, then, well,
   don't do it – it's as simple as that!

   I call this the *"connect the dots"* approach, where recognition
   is given within prescribed "dots." If we could change this
   mindset and ditch this approach, recognizing "outside of the
   dots" through "in the moment" recognition, then timely and
   frequent recognition will naturally happen and we'll make
   huge strides in closing the appreciation gap.

Gratitude has the power to energize

"Some leaders think it is necessary to withhold positive sentiments at
times in order to keep pressure on team members. Pressure like that
increases anxiety, and anxiety undermines productivity. In comparison,
research from Robert Emmons of the University of California, Davis, shows
that a leader who is more grateful amid difficult circumstances can help
people cope. As he explains, 'In the face of demoralization, gratitude has
the power to energize. In the face of brokenness, gratitude has the power
to heal. In the face of despair, gratitude has the power to bring hope.'"

Leading with Gratitude, by Adrian Gostick and Chester Elton

The importance of timely recognition

So why is "in the moment" recognition important? To answer this
question, let me share with you three things that could happen if it
does not occur:

1. **We miss important moments.**
   Think of an infant. We don't just celebrate birthdays, but
   celebrate all of the wonderful things they do in between – first
   steps, first words, etc. Why do we do that? It's because these

are also important moments and milestones, and ones that need to be celebrated and recognized in the moment. If we wait until their birthday, the individual moments get rolled into one, they lose their impact, and we miss the opportunity to celebrate and recognize these important achievements.

Another way of looking at it is like a board game. **When you recognize someone they move one step forward, and if you miss the recognition moment, they move one step backward**. Not good for your people and certainly not good for your company!

Winning isn't everything

In Deloitte's *The practical magic of 'thank you,'* they have a section titled "Winning isn't everything," where they share data about what people prefer to be recognized for. The highest score is for success (40%), however, it's interesting to see that 24% said it is for knowledge or expertise and 20% for effort. This says to me, and quite frankly it's no surprise, that people want to be appreciated and recognized for a variety of contributions.

As they say in the report, "End results matter, but the whole process is equally important and must be recognized. Results have many other parameters, but our efforts during the process are completely ours, hence, speaks more about us."

---

2. **We stifle performance.**
   Related to the last point, and continuing with the infant analogy, if we miss recognition moments our infant is not encouraged to keep going after those important moments. They think to themself, why bother, my parent didn't notice so why should I put any effort into learning new things?

   I know I've felt this way myself when I've failed to be recognized for going above and beyond to help someone or work on a project, thinking to myself, is it worth it? I know it sounds bad, but we're human, and as said at the start, we have basic needs to be valued and appreciated.

Timely recognition puts the foot on the accelerator

Let me ask you a question – if you were on a highway and the speed limit was 70 miles per hour, would you go this speed? The obvious answer is yes. If it was safe to do so and your car could drive that fast, of course you would, as it's what would get you to your destination the fastest.

What does this have to do with recognition? Well, if you had employees who you knew could do better and quicker work because they were recognized, as the data shows in Chapter 1, would you wait to give them this power, this speed, through recognition?

Of course you wouldn't, which means that by giving timely recognition your employees can put their foot on the accelerator. And, more importantly, keep their "car" – your company – driving forward.

---

3. **We lose the impact.**

   In my book *Build it: The Rebel Playbook for Employee Engagement*, my co-author Glenn Elliott tells the story of how in his first job he was recognized for his contributions by being told that he was being nominated for an award. He thought this was great, as it showed that he was noticed and appreciated. However, he goes on to say that it was over a year before he actually received the award, which by then he had completely forgotten why he had been nominated, and the impact was completely lost.

   I've heard this happen time and time again when we make our employees wait to be recognized. I see these as wasted opportunities and in the "why bother" camp as it does little to make an impact through recognition.

Let me end this section with some data to bring these points to life, further helping you should you need to convince your business partners to move in this direction. The first piece of data shows that employees want continuous recognition, and the second shows the gap, as they are not getting it:

- 80% of employees[23] said they feel recognition should happen on a continuous, all-year-round basis.

- Only 41% of employees[24] said they are recognized at their preferred frequency.

The next two pieces of data show the positive impact that timely and frequent recognition has on a company, showing the difference it can make between those doing it and those who are not:

- 14% more likely[25] to have better employee engagement, productivity and customer service with timely recognition.

- 41% more likely[26] to see increased employee retention with timely recognition.

Getting the timing right

Now that I've highlighted the reason for change, let me end this section by sharing four things to consider doing to make your recognition program more timely and frequent. Let me say upfront that I know from experience that these changes can be difficult to make based on what's been ingrained in your culture and/or your ways of working, but remember that any small step or change can make a big difference!

1. **Make sure you have some kind of "in the moment" recognition.**
   It's important to have at least one element of your recognition be "in the moment" recognition. Whether that's with e-cards or another vehicle, it's critical to have this so that your people don't have to wait to feel appreciated and your business doesn't have to wait to reap the benefits of recognition.

---

23 Study done by Reward Gateway.
24 Study done by Achievers.
25 Study done by Bersin by Deloitte.
26 Study done by Brandon Hall Group.

2. **Recognize small wins.**

   A key element of "in the moment" recognition is recognizing the small wins, those that work together and build up to create the big wins. Here's a lovely story from the book *Leading with Gratitude* that illustrates this concept:

   "Former Ford chief Alan Mulally explained to us that rewarding small wins shows that a leader knows what's going on. In his weekly business plan review, each member of his leadership team was expected to present a color-coded update of his or her progress toward meeting key company goals. When someone shows a red, we say, 'Thank you for that visibility.' When we work a red to a yellow, we thank everybody. Celebrations for each step show the team that it's expected behavior to make progress. People are feeling 'Wow. I'm needed. I'm supported.'"

3. **Revisit your time-based recognition programs.**

   If you have time-based recognition programs, which include annual, quarterly and monthly ones, I'd suggest that you revisit them to better understand their "reason for being," e.g. what are you trying to achieve through these? When doing this, challenge yourself to see if there are opportunities to shorten the timeframe or remove them entirely. Ask yourself, by having this program does it cause any of the problems that I've shared in this section? If it doesn't, great, but if it does, make some changes.

4. **Challenge yourself to revisit your years of service time frames.**

   And finally, if you have years of service programs, or what many call "long service" programs, it's important to revisit the existing time frames you are using. Companies have been changing their strategy and approach to these programs, moving from a way to recognize tenure to a way to celebrate ongoing contributions and careers, reflecting how years of service trends are changing.

Look at the time frames of your years of service awards and make sure that they reflect both your tenure and the recognition culture that you are trying to create. Personally, I'm a big fan of celebrating years of service every year, sending an anniversary e-card to mark the occasion in the same way as you do a birthday.

"If you don't show appreciation to those that deserve it, they'll learn to stop doing the things that you appreciate." Oyindamola Ademolu (m.o.j)

Calls to Action:

Evaluate how you currently train your leaders, managers and workforce on how recognition is given in a **meaningful way.** Answer the following questions and create a plan for each as required:

Do we effectively train our workforce on how to write a meaningful message? If not, how and when will we change our training?

Do we effectively train our workforce on how to understand and respect differences in what we say and do when recognition is given? If not, how and when will we change our training?

Do we recognize against our company values? If not, how and when will we make this change?

Evaluate how you currently design and deliver your recognition programs in a **unified and inclusive way,** listing any opportunities you have to do it better:

Do we let everyone give recognition? If not, what is holding us back from doing this?

Do we let everyone receive recognition? If not, what is holding us back from doing this?

Are there hurdles or obstacles in place that need to be overcome so that recognition can happen universally?

Evaluate how you currently put your recognition **under the spotlight,** listing any opportunities you have to do it better:

Doing well now:

Opportunities to improve:

Evaluate how you currently do **timely and frequent recognition,** keeping in mind the three things mentioned in the section, listing any opportunities you have to do it better:

Doing well now:

Opportunities to improve:

Chapter 3: Building your recognition pyramid

Chapter objectives

In this chapter, we'll cover:

- Why and how it's important to determine and set your recognition objectives.

- Why and how it's important to set recognition principles to help guide you to achieving your objectives.

- How to determine the "right" number of levels for your recognition pyramid.

- How to design your individual recognition plans, answering the key questions of "who," "when" and "what."

- How to work out the details of your recognition program and plans, including how you'll manage, communicate, train and measure them.

- Why and how to design your recognition branding, including the names and images to help you tell and market your recognition story.

Introduction

Now that we've gone through the basics of recognition and I've shared some guiding principles, it's time to roll up our sleeves and start exploring how to build or rebuild your recognition program. To help you with this, I'll be sharing a model called the "recognition pyramid," which is a model I was first introduced to when I was rebuilding our global recognition program at Reward Gateway. Since then, I've tweaked it to align with principles and lessons I learned over the years and now use time and time again as a tool to help organizations visualize and develop recognition programs. I look forward to sharing it with you, and having it help you meet your recognition and business objectives.

A recognition pyramid covers both the depth and breadth of appreciation, providing a comprehensive and complementary way to capture all of the moments that matter.

As you go through this chapter, keep in mind that each company's recognition pyramid should be different as they're designed based on factors such as your size, demographics, objectives, culture, values and even budget. To bring this point to life, in Chapter 5 I've shared lots of examples of pyramids, built by companies of different sizes, industries and countries. Together, I hope this helps you build a strong and powerful pyramid, one that will meet the current and future needs of your people and your business.

Here are the six steps I'll be going through in this chapter to help you design and build your recognition pyramid:

1	2	3
Determine your recognition objectives	Set your recognition principles	Determine the number of levels

4	5	6
Design your recognition plans	Decide how your recognition plans will work	Design your recognition branding

 Please note that throughout the chapter I've sprinkled what I call "rebel challenges," which are where I'll be asking you to put on your rebel cape and challenge your current practices and ways of thinking. You'll know it's a rebel challenge when you see this icon appearing in a box. Go for it!

1. Determine your recognition objectives

The first step is to set your recognition strategy by determining your objectives. You do this by answering the question "why"– why do you want and need to recognize your workforce? This will give you the target to aim for as you develop your individual recognition plans. Or, as Simon Sinek, author of *Start With Why*, says, "When you start with why in everything that you do, you inspire action in a way that what doesn't."

Here are four things to consider as you determine your recognition objectives:

1. **Your company's mission, values and culture.**
   The starting point is to align your recognition strategy with your company's mission, values and culture. This will help you achieve your overall vision and goals (your mission), the actions and behaviors you desire (your values), and reflect who you are as a company (your culture). Do this and all the "pieces" fit together in a cohesive picture and direction. If you don't, there will be confusion and a lack of focus.

   According to research[27] by SHRM and Workhuman, **70% of companies tie their recognition programs to their company values**.

2. **Your business and people objectives.**
   Next, you want to align your recognition strategy with your business and people objectives. For example, do you have objectives based around developing new products to focus your workforce on innovation? Do you have people objectives around developing stronger teams to focus your workforce on collaboration? Consider these when developing your recognition strategy so that it reinforces and drives employees to meet these objectives.

   According to research by Bersin & Associates, **60% of companies tie their recognition programs to business goals**.

---

27   2018 study done by SHRM and Workhuman.

3. **Your business and people challenges.**
   Next, it's important to align your recognition strategy with any business and people challenges that you may have. For example, is engagement, productivity, and/or retention a problem that could be positively impacted by your recognition plan? Consider these as you develop your strategy and individual programs so that they become a strength and not a weakness.

4. **Your reward strategy.**
   And finally, it's important to align your recognition strategy with your overall reward strategy. Since recognition is just one element of your rewards, along with pay, benefits, incentives, etc., it's critical that they all work together, completing the total rewards picture and objectives.

After taking this all into account, you should be able to answer the question "why" and develop your recognition objectives.

Common recognition objectives

According to the 2020 State of Recognition Report, the five most common objectives of recognition programs are to:

1. Increase employee engagement – 88%
2. Create a culture of recognition – 86%
3. Reduce employee turnover – 63%
4. Create consistency and/or transparency – 55%
5. Improve cross-functional and communication – 42%

Here are other examples of recognition objectives:

- Improve teamwork, collaboration and connections
- Encourage and reinforce a high-performance culture
- Encourage and reinforce a learning culture
- Motivate teams to deliver against specific business criteria

---

2. Set your recognition principles

Now that you've answered the critical "why" question, you have one more thing to do before moving on to build your recognition program, and that is to create your recognition principles. These are what help you define your program, what it stands for, what makes it unique and what it says to your employees and the external marketplace. Finding the right principles will help you create recognition plans which truly drive and support your "why," aligning with your company's mission, values and culture.

You may be wondering, what is the difference between your recognition objectives and principles? Your objectives are high-level, and your principles are the next level. Your principles need to guide the design of your recognition program so that your recognition objectives are met. They are both important, and need to be determined and set up front.

When designing your principles, I always suggest starting with your mission and values to ensure that your principles are strengthening your overall company vision. To illustrate this, let me share with you the recognition principles we developed at Reward Gateway before we began redesigning our recognition program, showing how they fit and work together alongside the company's mission and values.

Mission: Let's make the world a better place to work.			
Values:			
We love our job	We are human	We delight our customers	We work hard
We own it	We push the boundaries	We speak up	We think global
Recognition Principles:			
Fairness	Balance	Wow	Easy

Let me end by suggesting that **before** you finalize your recognition objectives and principles, that you get input from your key business partners to give them the opportunity to contribute and help set the direction. You should also get input after you've drafted them to ensure continual buy-in.

3. Determine the number of levels

It's now time to start building your recognition pyramid, and where you'll be getting into the nitty-gritty details by answering the important questions of "what," "who" and "how." But before you do this, you need to build the framework of your pyramid and determine the number of levels that it will have. Think of it as a blueprint for your program – the clearer the levels are in your pyramid, the more successful it will be in helping you achieve your objectives.

So without further ado, here is the recognition pyramid model.

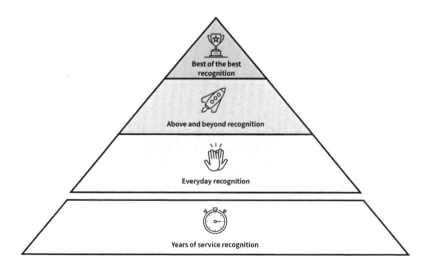

You'll notice that there are three primary levels of the pyramid, and one level for years of service that sits outside of the other levels. The reason for this is that although recognizing for years of service is a common form of recognition, and a way to make employees feel appreciated for their contributions to the company, it does not directly relate to specific actions, behaviors and impacts, which the others do. For this reason, I believe it is best to leave it as a separate and standalone level, not trying to squeeze it under one of your other levels or recognition plans.

Here are high level definitions for the four levels of the recognition pyramid:

- **The "everyday" level** – The bottom level of the pyramid, the widest part, is "everyday" recognition, and is typically given by anyone at any time for day-to-day accomplishments and achievements. For this reason, it touches the most employees as it happens the most frequently. It recognizes moments that, although important, are of *low impact*, meaning they impact a small number of people and/or customers with minimal impact to them and with little extra work and effort required.

- **The "above and beyond" level** – Here is where the pyramid starts getting a bit narrower, symbolizing how fewer employees would typically receive this type of recognition as it's harder to reach this level of achievement. It recognizes moments that are of *higher impact*, meaning where employees or teams have excelled, going above and beyond to get the job done. Think of it as a ladder, with employees needing to work that much harder to get to the next rung of the ladder, which in this case is your recognition plan.

- **The "best of the best" level** – The top level of the pyramid symbolizes those who went above and beyond the most – often outside of their typical job role – symbolizing performing at the highest level within your organization. It recognizes moments that are of the *highest impact*, having a larger or more long-term impact on a group or the business, requiring more work and effort to accomplish this. Again, think of it as a ladder, but this time think of the bell at the top that you ring when you get to the very top.

- **Years of service level** – This level of the pyramid as explained earlier sits outside of the primary levels of the pyramid, and is used to recognize employees for hitting certain key tenure milestones.

Now before you ask me how many levels there should be in your pyramid, let me say that there is no perfect or magic number, the key here is to come up with the number of levels that will ultimately help you meet your recognition objectives. If it takes one level to do this, great! And if it's four, that's fine as well.

Companies have varying numbers of levels in their recognition pyramid

The plays in Chapter 5 will show how each company has built their recognition pyramid differently, using some or all of the four levels. But to further illustrate this point, let me share with you data from the survey[28] I conducted for this book, where I asked companies to name the levels that they had within their own recognition programs (pyramids). Here's what they reported back:

- Everyday recognition – 84%
- Above and beyond recognition – 78%
- Best of the best recognition – 66%
- Years of service recognition – 83%

Say/do exercise

The approach I developed and have used with organizations to determine the number of primary levels in a recognition pyramid is what I call the "say/do" exercise, which is when you bring your people together in sessions to help understand and see recognition through their eyes. The task you will have them do is to think of and write down all of the times when they have given recognition, felt they should have, or could possibly do so in the future. They could be based on activities (e.g., joining the company, having a work anniversary or birthday) or based on actions (e.g., helping a customer, helping a team member or suggesting a new way of doing things), and reflect on the moments where your employees are asking for or the business requires recognition to take place.

---

28 To download a free copy of the full survey results, go to www.debcohr.com/free-resources

For each of these recognition moments, ask them to write down these things:

- **The impact** – There are two parts to this, the first being **who** was impacted by the action or behavior, e.g. me, the team, the company, etc., and second, **how** they were impacted by it. Ask them to provide as much detail as possible as it will help you later determine the number of levels.

- **The say and do** – Next, for each moment have them write down what they said and did, or would have wanted to say and do to make their colleague(s) feel appreciated and recognized for their actions. Again, the more detail the better, as it can help you understand the differences between situations which will ultimately help you design your program and individual plans.

To illustrate this exercise, here are a few examples:

Moment	Impact		Say/do
	Who	**How**	
A colleague came in an hour early to cover my shift.	Me	I could take my child to school, which was important to me.	I sent a note to thank them for helping me, living our value "teamwork."
A colleague not scheduled to work, came in at the last minute to run a client event in place of a sick colleague.	Me Client	The client was able to hold this important event, making our company look good to them.	I gave them a note along with a bottle of their favorite wine.
A colleague from another team helped us for a month to finish a project.	Team Client	We were able to finish the project on time, meeting the client's needs.	We all signed a card that was delivered along with a voucher to a local restaurant.
An employee came up with an idea to save the company money.	Company	Because of their proactive and hard work for three months, they saved the company money.	CEO sent them a handwritten thank you note along with a voucher to stay at a hotel for a weekend.

Once they've done this, either they or you can map the recognition moments into the three levels of the recognition pyramid, which is what you'll do in the next step to develop your individual recognition plans. My favorite way to do this is with a Post-it exercise, either in person or virtually, where you put each moment on a Post-it and put it under the recognition level on the wall.

The result of this exercise is to have an understanding of whether you need some or all of these three levels in your recognition pyramid. You decide this based on what appears under each level and also what you think needs to fit under it to meet all of your recognition objectives. Remember, these three levels are just a starting point!

4. Design your recognition plans

Once you've decided on your recognition levels, the next step is to design your individual recognition plans. To do this, you'll need to determine the "what," "who" and "when" for each of your recognition levels. As you go through this, it will help you decide if you need one recognition plan per level or multiple ones. The key is to take your time to thoroughly answer these questions, constantly referring back to the recognition moments collected from the say/do exercise, getting input and feedback along the way, and keeping in mind your overall recognition objectives.

Connect the dots

Earlier in the book I said that connecting the dots was a negative, explaining it as recognizing only at certain times, or "dots," and not "in the moment." However, I'd now like to define it in a different context, explaining it this time as a positive, something to keep in mind as you design your recognition plans. It is absolutely critical to remind yourself that recognition is just one tool you have to show appreciation and drive engagement. As you design your program and the individual plans, it's important to look across them as well as your entire reward proposition to understand how they all work (or don't work) together, making sure that you "connect the dots." Going back to a study mentioned in the Introduction, the last thing you want to do is to deliver a program that makes your employees feel that it is taking the place of compensation or any other reward element.

Before we begin answering these key decisions, let me share with you the three most common types of recognition plans:

- **Peer-to-peer** – According to the "2020 State of Recognition Report," **66% of companies have some kind of peer-to-peer recognition plan**, where colleagues are able to give recognition to each other. They have been proven to have a positive impact on a company's financial performance, with a SHRM study finding them being 36% more likely to have a positive impact on financial recognition over manager only recognition, and also on team culture, with a study by O.C. Tanner[29] showing that it increases the probability of a constructive team culture by 2.5 times.

- **Years of service** – According to the "2020 State of Recognition Report," **61% of companies have some kind of years of service recognition plan**, where employees are recognized for hitting certain service milestones. According to a survey by O.C. Tanner, they foster feelings of appreciation, with 81% of employees surveyed saying that career celebrations help them feel appreciated for their work.

- **Quarterly and/or annual awards** – And finally, according to the "2020 State of Recognition Report," **37% of companies have some kind of quarterly and/or annual recognition award**, which are given to individuals or teams at certain times throughout the year for being the best-of-the best, reflecting their contributions and impact above and beyond others. These programs differ based on when they happen, how many winners there are, and even the nomination process for selecting winners.

Determine the "what"

Let's start by answering the question "what," which will help drive your reward and recognition strategy, as well as send a strong message to your employees about what is appreciated at your company, and how

---

29   O.C. Tanner's 2020 Global Culture Report.

their contributions are valued. There are two parts to this question, which I describe as the "in" and the "out." The "in" represents what goes into recognition, so what needs to happen to be recognized. The "out" represents what goes out of recognition, so what the person recognized will receive when they are recognized. They are both important to answer, and both have a huge impact on the ultimate design of your recognition plans.

As you answer your questions, I suggest that you refer back to the responses you had during the say/do exercise. This will give you an idea of what is important to them and the business, and will guide you as you make your recognition plan design decisions.

What are you trying to recognize?

The first question to ask is what is your company trying to recognize? What are the actions and behaviors that you believe should be recognized, and how do they fit within your different recognition levels and individual plans? As described above, this is the "in," so what opens the door to recognition, giving your employees the opportunity to be recognized. This should reflect what is important to your company based on your desired recognition culture and recognition objectives.

As you answer this question, here are some considerations:

1. **Decide if/how you will incorporate your values.**
   In Chapter 2, I spoke about the power of recognizing against your company values, and that by doing this you are two times more likely to reinforce and drive business results and four times more likely to have your employees say that they believe in your values. For these reasons, when you decide what will "open the door" to recognition, I'd suggest considering using your company values as one of your key levers. As you'll see in the plays in Chapter 5, the majority of companies I interviewed do exactly this. And if you don't have formal values, that's OK, encourage recognition to be based on actions and behaviors you want your employees to take, which could in the future become your company values.

2. **Decide what you will do to recognize small and big wins.**

   In Chapter 2, I spoke about the importance of recognizing both small and big wins. This is critical to consider when you answer the question "what," and this is why I see many companies put these small, but important wins in the entry-level recognition plans as shown in the following table. You'll need to decide what a small step and small win looks like at your company, and then put it in the appropriate recognition plan(s).

3. **Decide if/how you will recognize effort over results.**

   There are some situations which are called "learning moments" (a term taught to me by the CEO of WD-40 Garry Ridge), when things don't go exactly as planned, but where our employees still walk away having learned an important lesson. You'll need to decide if these actions warrant a recognition, recognizing the effort over the results. Some companies I've spoken to have done this, putting this "what" in their entry-level recognition plan. For example, if your professional development culture is one where you discuss how to learn from failures as well as successes, then this should be woven into your recognition program as well.

4. **Decide if/how you'll recognize years of service.**

   As you'll notice, in the say/do exercise I didn't mention years of service as it sits below the primary levels of your recognition pyramid. But since it is a common and often important part of your recognition strategy, it's important to decide if you want to recognize years of service, and regarding the "what," think about the reason for doing so, which will help you decide the "when" regarding the timing, e.g. every year, every five years, etc.

5. **Figure out how you will capture silent or unsung heroes.**

   When I speak to employees about recognition, one of the biggest complaints I hear from them is that they feel there is not an opportunity for everyone to be recognized. These are often the silent or unsung heroes, the ones who may work in a department that may not be under the spotlight, or work on projects that get little notice. As I said at the start, every employee deserves to be recognized, so it's important to consider the "what" that these people are doing, not leaving them out by ignoring their important contributions.

6. **Make it clear so that you recognize fairly and consistently.**
    And finally, as you define the "what" consider how you will communicate them so that they are clear to your people and so that recognition can happen in a fair and consistent manner. I always think of this as I'm developing the "what," making sure that as I go through the process I am able to explain and defend them. If I can't, then I change them.

    One way to help employees understand the "what" before recognizing it is something they've done at LinkedIn (see play in Chapter 5). They have built into their online recognition system an "award advisor" that asks employees a series of questions to assist and guide the employee to the most appropriate award based on the scope and impact of the contributions. This helps employees self-educate on how to recognize in the most meaningful and effective way as they complete their award nomination.

It's important to point out that for each level of your recognition pyramid, the "what" will most likely differ, for as mentioned in the previous section, the impact increases as you go up the pyramid. Here are some examples to illustrate this point, but do keep in mind that this will differ from company to company based on your business, your goals and ultimately what impact means to you:

Level 1	Level 2	Level 3
Everyday recognition	**Above and beyond recognition**	**Best of the best recognition**
• Welcome a new employee • Help out a colleague or customer • Share knowledge and expertise • Solve a problem • Quickly turn around a request • Learn a new skill • Hit a goal or milestone	• Achieve an important goal • Present an innovative idea • Solve a complex problem • Overcome a big challenge • Spot ways to increase safety	• Develop a new process that improves productivity or saves the company money • Drive an important/critical project that is outside the scope of your job

What recognition rewards are "right"?

The second part of the "what" is when you decide what will come "out" of a recognition moment, so what will you do to reward your employees under each of your individual recognition plans? In Chapter 2 I spoke about the words and the messages that come out of recognition, but here I want to focus on the actions that come out of recognition. This is an area that has changed over the years, with companies getting more strategic and creative in what they do, moving away from the easy choice of money or a few gifts to options that align with their culture, values and employer brand.

For me, this is where the magic, or the damage, happens, as it's critical to get these decisions right for your program to succeed. To illustrate this, let me share two stories, one with a happy ending and one with, well, let's just say that it didn't end as we had planned. For both, I'll share what we did with our awards and what our employees did with their actions.

- In Company A we rewarded employees with points, or money, to use through our online discount platform, with them deciding when and how they wanted to use them. My all-time favorite story from an employee on how they spent their points was when one told me of how he had saved up all of the small individual recognition awards to buy a pair of shoes through the discount platform. And (this is the part I love!), he said that every time he walked in the shoes he thought of all of the people who had appreciated him.

- In Company B we had come up with the idea of having special watches designed as a way to thank people for their time, for their years of service. The watches were absolutely lovely and could not be bought in a store, or so we thought as we unfortunately came to find out that some of our employees were selling them on eBay as they didn't want them. What a shame!

9 tips for getting your recognition rewards "right"

So how do you get it right, create that magic for your employees, and achieve that ROI (return on investment) for your company? Here are nine things to think about and address to help you with this:

1. **Make it meaningful.**
   Going back to our MUST acronym, the first thing to think about is how your rewards can be meaningful, e.g. relevant, important and valuable to them. It might seem obvious, of course we want them to be meaningful, but too often companies fail to understand their people and give out awards that lack meaning and thus impact. For example, look at what happened with the watch in the previous note. We saw by the actions of some employees, they saw no meaning and value from this reward as they didn't want and/or need it.

Always, always, always, start by listening to and understanding what matters and is meaningful to your employees, and you'll have a better chance of your rewards being right for them.

For example, at many companies handing out certificates to recognize employees just doesn't work, with employees not feeling appreciated by this act as it could be deemed a bit old-fashioned. However, as shared in the University of Lincoln play, a key part of one of their recognition plans is for their vice-chancellor to present recognition recipients with a certificate during their annual awards ceremony. This has meaning because it is something they do with their students to symbolize their achievements and contributions and thus it delivers the same meaning and impact to their staff. What works for one company or organization might not work for another, which is why it's important to get feedback from your employees from the start.

2. **Think about the connections.**
   Build a connection and relationship between the reward you give (or don't give) and the impact of the actions and behaviors. For example, in Chapter 2, I shared a story of when a business partner wanted to give a member of my team $1,000 for the support they had given them during the annual pay review process. By doing this there would have been a disconnect between their actions and the reward, for as I had explained, this was part of their job and thus their efforts and the impact were not above and beyond what was expected. By giving this reward it would have not only sent the wrong message to the employee (and the rest of my team), but it could have caused problems in the future as they would have expected similar rewards for similar actions going forward.

3. **Consider the relationships.**
   Ask yourself, how do rewards for one recognition plan compare to rewards for another one, either at a lower or higher level in the recognition pyramid? These relationships are based on the impact of the actions and behaviors and going back to the concept of steps between recognition levels

and plans as I explained earlier, it's important to look at the relative step from one plan to another.

For example, at one company when we looked at the relationships we saw a big jump from one recognition plan to the next recognition plan in our pyramid, so we doubled the reward from one to the other. However, at the next level plan, we saw a smaller jump, so the reward was only slightly higher. The key here is to understand, map out and then address these "jumps" as you determine your rewards.

4. **Consider the relationships to other reward programs.**
   The other relationship to consider as you develop your recognition rewards is in respect to your other elements of reward, e.g. pay, bonuses, incentives. The reason I suggest reviewing this is that often I've seen companies where the recognition reward is the same if not more than an annual bonus award. In these situations, you need to ask yourself – is the level of contribution for both the same? Often the answer is no, as an annual bonus is for work achieved throughout the year, where a recognition reward is often for a shorter time frame and effort. Bottom line, review them together to ensure they connect, align and fit together into a cohesive total rewards package.

5. **Consider offering choice.**
   Over the years, more and more companies are offering their employees choice when they receive their recognition awards. The benefits of this is that it lets them decide what will make them feel appreciated, respecting their individual preferences and the overall diversity of your workforce. A common way to do this as you'll see in the data in the next section and also in the plays in Chapter 5 are with gift cards and points through an online recognition platform. This lets your employees decide when and how they want to use them, putting decision-making in their hands.

6. **Find a balance.**
   Besides choice, another key element of effective recognition programs is balance, especially when there's so much

diversity in our workforce and in the work that is being done. And when it comes to recognition rewards, this is absolutely key, trying to strike that perfect balance between financial and non-financial rewards and formal and informal recognition. Check out the examples in Chapter 5 for ideas and inspiration.

"People wrongly think they need to choose one over the other, but the truth is your employees need both non-financial recognition and financial recognition and rewards, with great programs having a mix of both. Non-financial reinforces progress, keeps people motivated and supports teams to build connection and camaraderie. Financial helps organizations signal to the employee that their action/behavior has made a significant impact on business objectives and organizational goals and is highly valued." Kylie Terrell, Director of Consultancy, Reward Gateway Australia.

7. **Do it your own way.**
   The next thing to ask yourself is, how can you design recognition rewards in your unique way? In Chapter 5 you'll see examples of how companies have done this, but I thought I'd share more examples from my other books to further help and inspire you:

   - **T-shirts** – At Nav, a U.S. FinTech company, they give out t-shirts that display the value they are being recognized for. As Levi King, CEO & Co-Founder explained to me, "We're not a workplace of plaques and certificates, we are t-shirt kind of people."

   - **Miniature wagon** – At Radio Flyer, an American toy company best known for their popular red toy wagon, they give out golden wagons, which are miniature replicas of one of their products, as a way to recognize one another for living their company values. The wagons are passed from one employee to another each month along with a handwritten "you are awesome" note. The recipient of the wagon adds their initials on the bottom of the wagon before passing it onto the next person.

- **Golden toilet** – At Venables Bell & Partner, a U.S. marketing agency, they have a bit of fun with their annual awards, creating ones that are fun and quirky, aligning with their culture. One example is their golden toilet award that is given to the employee who "takes care of shit gracefully and with class," explained Paul Venables, Founder & CEO, with the winner receiving a full-size golden toilet.

- **Once-in-a-lifetime trip** – At Dishoom, a U.K. restaurant group, to recognize and celebrate employees for their five-year anniversary, they are invited to join the co-founders and their Executive Chef on a trip to Bombay for a "Bombay Bootcamp." This once-in-a-lifetime trip is not only a reward for years of selfless service but a complete immersion in the company's heritage and culture.

- **Name a star** – At Virgin Group, the umbrella group for Virgin businesses, all employees who are recognized as part of their group "Star of the Year" program have a star named after them. This not only creates a lasting memory, but truly makes them feel like a star.

- **Badges** – At KidZania, an indoor city designed for children, employees can receive a recognition badge that has a logo of one of their values as a way to recognize one another. Once awarded, they are proudly pinned on the lanyard that employees wear around their necks for all to see.

8. **Understand the implications.**
   It's important to pay attention to, understand and then address the implications and impact of your rewards. Here are two examples that immediately come to mind:

   - **Tax implications** – The first has to do with the tax implications, so employees being taxed for receiving their recognition rewards. By doing this, I've seen it cause surprise, frustration, anger, or a combination of all of them. A hilarious and yet sad story illustrating this was shared in a blog[30] I read by Karen Eber where she tells of a broken recognition trophy she received. When telling her manager that it was broken, she was sent a replacement one, which again arrived broken. What also arrived were two separate emails telling her that she was being taxed for not just one but for both of the trophies. She ends her blog by saying "I came away annoyed, less engaged and having learned to not volunteer on future projects." The moral of this story is not just about making sure your gifts are sent intact but to make sure that your approach to tax doesn't "shatter" the recognition experience.

According to a survey[31] conducted in 2019 by WorldatWork representing around 500 companies in North America, almost half of them (46%) increase the valued amount of the recognition award to offset the tax impact (also known as grossing up the award). This shows that some do and some don't pay the tax on behalf of the recognition award. My personal preference is to pay the tax even if it means a slightly lower reward amount as it makes it a better overall experience for my employees. However, if you decide not to do this so that there are no surprises, I suggest you clearly explain upfront how the taxation will work for employee

- **Procurement implications** – The second has to do with employees not being able to redeem a reward, so there are problems with the procurement, getting and receiving them. I've seen this happen in a few different ways. The first example happened when I worked for an American company that would send rewards from the U.S. to other companies. It made sense from a procurement perspective as it meant they could order in bulk and manage the process centrally. However, stories of toasters catching on fire or televisions not working, made us soon realize that this just would not work.

---

30 Appeared in a blog titled "The Broken Trophy" on kareneber.com.
31 2019 "Trends in Recognition" report conducted by WorldatWork and Maritz Motivation.

The second example happened when we went with a global supplier who told us that they could support our employees in all countries with our point-based recognition program. It sounded great until I had my HR Director in Israel call to tell me that for most of the gifts and experiences they had to either travel to another country to redeem it or wait months and months for it to arrive.

Both of these are situations you want to avoid, so think through if there are these or any other procurement issues that could happen as a result of the rewards you select and the processes you create.

9. **Remember, it's not about the money!**
   Last, but certainly not least, is to make the point that it is never, ever, ever all about the money when it comes to deciding your recognition "what." As you'll see in the data in the next section, most employees prefer non-financial over financial recognition. What this says and means is that we need to focus on getting the foundations of recognition right first, making sure that the first reward is the reward of being recognized, and then if it's right, the second reward can have a financial value.

Rebel challenge – get your recognition rewards "right"

My challenge to you is to use the nine tips I've just shared to honestly assess your current recognition rewards to determine if they are right. If they fall short on any of these, be brave and look at how you can change them to tick the box and meet the needs of your people and your recognition program.

How others are rewarding recognition

It's now time to share with you what others are doing regarding their recognition rewards. I intentionally had this follow the previous section as I didn't want you to just take what others are doing and run with it.

Instead, I wanted you to start by thinking about what is right for your company and your people, regardless of what others are doing, and then use the following data as a litmus test and/or for further inspiration.

The first pieces of data show **what employees want**:

- A study conducted by Deloitte[32] asked employees how they would prefer to be recognized for day-to-day accomplishments. The results were that 85% said they wanted either a verbal or written thank you, with only 7% saying they wanted a celebration or gift.

- A study by Reward Gateway[33] found that 72% of employees said a simple thank you would make them feel more motivated and help build morale.

- The Motivating by Appreciation (MBA) Inventory[34], which contains data from over 100,000 respondents, shows that employees' first choices for being shown appreciation are as follows:

  - Words of affirmation – 47%
  - Quality time (e.g. time with others, working together) – 25%
  - Acts of service (e.g. assisting a colleague in getting work done) – 22%
  - Tangible gifts – 6%

The data consistently shows that employees prefer non-financial rewards, a thank you, over gifts. However, I think it's important to point out from what I've seen over the years when talking to and surveying my employees is that expectations change as you move up the recognition pyramid. In these situations, as more effort and impact goes into the recognition actions, I've seen employees expecting something more to make them feel appreciated and valued. This could still be non-financial, e.g. development opportunities, or it could be financial, but

---

32 2019 study done by Deloitte.
33 2017 study done by Reward Gateway.
34 2017 research by Dr. Paul White, Appreciation at Work.

the key is to understand both what your people want and balance it with your recognition strategy.

The second pieces of data show what rewards **companies are giving**:

- A study conducted by WorldatWork[35] reported the following recognition rewards are being given:

  - Gift cards – 62%
  - Cash – 50%
  - Clocks/Watches – 49%
  - Trophies/Plaques/Certificates – 47%
  - Apparel/Accessories – 46%
  - Jewelry – 46%

- A study conducted by Achievers[36] reported the following recognition rewards are being given:

  - Gift cards – 74%
  - Merchandise chosen by employee – 55%
  - Company-branded merchandise – 37%
  - Cash – 36%
  - Predetermined products – 34%
  - Organized trips and events – 32%

The data consistently shows that gift cards are the most common form of recognition reward being given, and from here there is a variety of other forms of reward. It's important to point out that as you review this data, keep in mind that many of the rewards reported in the surveys are for years of service programs, thus such a high percentage of traditional rewards such as clocks, watches, trophies, plaques, etc.

It's important to point out that for the data shared with you above, **all levels** of recognition are amalgamated in the survey results, so it doesn't distinguish between the different levels of the recognition pyramid. For the survey[37] conducted for this book, I asked participants

---

35   2019 "Trends in Recognition" report by WorldatWork and Maritz Motivation.

36   2020 "State of Recognition" report by Achievers

37   To download a free copy of the full survey results, go to www.debcohr.com/free-resources

which awards they give employees at each of the different levels of the recognition pyramid to see if/how awards differ. While gift cards and vouchers still remained at the top, my survey presented slightly different results. Here's an overview:

- **Everyday recognition**
  - 52% of companies surveyed provide non-financial recognition at this level, with the most common ways being e-Cards (69%), shout or call outs (20%), and handwritten notes or postcards (9%).

  - 48% of companies provide financial recognition at this level, many doing so by providing a variety of different awards. The most common ways are gift cards or vouchers (77%), company-branded merchandise (20%), attendance at an event (15%), money (14%), a paid day off (11%) and a plaque or trophy (9%).

- **Above and beyond recognition**
  - Only 6% of companies provide non-financial recognition at this level.

  - 94% of companies provide financial recognition at this level, many again doing so by providing a variety of different awards. The most common ways are gift cards or vouchers (64%), money (29%), gifts (11%), attendance at an event (10%), a plaque or trophy (9%), company-branded merchandise (8%), a paid day off (7%) and an experience (5%).

- **Above and beyond recognition**
  - Only 10% of companies provide non-financial recognition at this level.

  - 90% of companies provide financial recognition at this level, doing so by providing a variety of different awards. The most common ways are gift cards or vouchers (53%), money (39%), attendance at an event (20%), a plaque or trophy (14%), an experience (12%), company-branded merchandise (11%), a gift (7%) and a paid day off (6%).

- **Years of service recognition**
  - Only 8% of companies provide non-financial recognition at this level.

  - 82% of companies provide financial recognition at this level, doing so by providing a variety of different awards. The most common ways are gift cards or vouchers (42%), money (16%), a paid day off (16%), attendance at an event (11%), a plaque or trophy (11%), company-branded merchandise (11%), a gift (10%), a pin or badge (5%), an experience (4%), and a watch (4%).

Decide the "who"

The next question to answer is the "who," which is when you decide who will be able to give, receive and approve recognition and recognition awards. As I go through each of these three areas, keep in mind that the answers to the questions may differ from recognition plan to recognition plan, which is absolutely fine as the intent and goal of the plans will differ.

Who should give recognition?

First, you need to decide for each individual recognition plan who will be able to give recognition under it. Will it be everyone (peer-to-peer recognition), or will it be just your managers or leaders? As you'll see in the plays in Chapter 5, this often differs from plan to plan as you go up the recognition pyramid, with the entry level often being peer-to-peer, and later up the pyramid moving to manager- or leader-given recognition.

> Recognition coming from a manager can be effective at showing employees that they are seen and valued, while also giving them short- and long-term feedback to help them perform at their best throughout their career.
>
> According to a study[38] on motivation by McKinsey & Company, praise and commendation by your immediate manager is more motivating than performance- based cash bonuses, showing the power of manager recognition.

To illustrate this, here are a few examples from the plays in Chapter 5 showing who can give recognition at the different levels of the recognition pyramid:

Who can give recognition (by pyramid level)			
Company	Level 1 Everyday recognition	Level 2 Above & beyond recognition	Level 3 Best of the best recognition
Atlassian	Everyone	Everyone	Everyone
Heineken	Everyone	Managers	Everyone can nominate
Zoom	Everyone can nominate	Everyone can nominate	Leaders

When deciding who can and should give recognition, it's important to go back and look at the recognition moments shared in the say/do exercise and think about who best will be able to see these moments as they happen, and thus be able to recognize them through the plan.

---

38 Quarterly Study done by McKinsey & Company, June 2009

Rebel challenge – increase the number of givers

My challenge to you is to look at any of your recognition plans that currently do not let your entire workforce participate, and ask yourself if there is a genuine reason to continue doing it this way? Could more people be givers in this program? Weigh the risks versus the benefits, and then decide what is best to drive recognition and support your people and your business.

Who should **receive** recognition?

Next, you need to decide who can and should receive recognition for each individual recognition plan. Again, it's important to look at the recognition moments and ask yourself two questions. First, will everyone have an equal opportunity to perform and achieve at this level or can only certain functions or job levels have the chance to earn this recognition? Second, will you have an open-ended approach to receiving recognition? For example, can anyone be recognized, or is it only a certain number or percentage that can be recognized under this plan at a specified time (e.g. five per month)?

Another part of this is deciding if recognition is given as individuals, teams or a combination of both. As more companies see the impact that teamwork can have on meeting their goals and objectives, they're developing team-based recognition plans, recognizing teams for their collective contributions and achievements, highlighting and encouraging successful teamwork across their workforce.

Teamwork keeps the ball in play

A study was done by BYU that found the ratio of assists (players passing the ball to one another) to turnovers (players losing the ball) is much more predictive of success. That's because turnovers mean players are hogging the ball so that they can score, whereas lots of assists mean the players aren't trying to make individual shots, they're trying to get the collective win.

Rebel challenge – increase the number of receivers

My challenge to you is to look at any of your recognition plans that currently focus on the best of the best, and ask yourself if there is a genuine reason to continue doing it this way? Could you have endless winners or does there need to be a limit? Could employees win against objectives and goals instead of against each other? Weigh the risks versus the benefits, and then decide what is best to drive recognition and support your people and your business.

Who should approve recognition?

And finally, if you decide to have recognition involving rewards, you'll need to decide who can and will approve each of these rewards. Can the person giving the reward do so, or does it need to go to someone else in the organization, e.g. Human Resources, the line manager, a director, etc?

I suggest you make these decisions by linking them back to your culture, values and objectives, or as I've said a few times already, you will have misalignment. For example, when I was putting in place a recognition program at a previous company I was ready to have peer-to-peer awards go to Human Resources for approval as this was what we had done at my previous company. However, when pausing to consider the disconnect this was to our culture and values, especially as the awards were only a value of $15, we decided to have no approval required, instead focusing on making sure that our workforce understood why and when these should be awarded.

Rebel challenge – reduce the number of approvers

My challenge to you is to look at any of your recognition plans that currently have approvers, and ask yourself if there is a genuine reason to continue doing it this way? Ask yourself, does this slow the process down and/or create mistrust with your people? Especially with awards of small levels, for the 5% of your employees who may use it in the wrong way, either intentionally or by mistake, is it worth having this rule for the 95% who will do the right thing? Weigh the risks versus the benefits, and then decide what is best to drive recognition and support your people and your business.

Decide the "when"

The next decision you'll have to make is the "when," which has to do with when employees will be recognized under each of your recognition plans. As with the "who," the "when" may differ from recognition plan to recognition plan, which again is absolutely fine.

You have two options with the "when":

- **Always on** – This is when recognition can be given at any time, thus your plan is "always on." At least for the entry level of the recognition pyramid, most companies have moved to this so that actions and behaviors can be captured and recognized "in the moment" similar to their approach to feedback.

- **Time-based** – The other option is recognition that happens at a specified period of time, e.g. monthly, quarterly or annual. This is commonly done for recognition higher up in the pyramid, especially when it involves a time-consuming process such as nominations.

Before making your decision for this, I suggest you look closely at the recognition moments to understand when they happen and when would be the most meaningful time to recognize them. For this, you may find the section in Chapter 2 about recognition timing helpful.

Rebel challenge – reduce the timing

My challenge to you is to look at any of your recognition plans that are time-bound, and ask yourself if there is a genuine reason to continue doing it this way? Will waiting to give the recognition make it more impactful or will it take away from this opportunity to show your employees that you appreciate them? Again, it's important here to weigh the risks versus the benefits, and then decide what is best for your organization.

How to handle nomination approvals

After you design your recognition plans, you may end up with some that involve nominations, e.g. employees are nominated to receive the recognition award and a certain number are selected. In these situations, there are some additional decisions that you'll need to make, which I've listed below:

- **How many will be selected?**
  You'll need to decide how many employees will ultimately be selected to receive the recognition under this plan. If your plan is to recognize against your company values, for example, will it be one recipient for each company value? Two? Or, will it be a certain number of recipients that live more than one value? Will there be a team award? Will there be any special business-related awards? Think about what this plan is intended to do, and based on this determine the right number to achieve its objectives.

- **Who will do the selection?**
  You'll also need to decide who will review and approve the nominations. The key is to select the "right" people at your company to do this, ones who have the right balance and blend of *knowledge* so they'll understand the business well enough to understand what is being recognized, and *impartiality*, so will not turn it into a popularity contest. If you don't get this right you end up having the wrong people selected for these awards and you create what I call the "eye-rollers," which are employees who roll their eyes every time a name is called out for receiving this recognition award as they

don't believe they deserve it. You need credibility and fairness in who selects and approves these awards, so take the time to pick the right people.

- **What happens to those not selected?**
  And finally, it's important to decide upfront what you will do with those that are not selected to receive the recognition award. The biggest mistake you can make is to do nothing, for there is still an opportunity to recognize them by sharing with these people the fact that people thought enough to nominate them, and then share the reasons for doing this.

How to handle years of service

The next decision to make is if/how to design your years of service level of your recognition pyramid. Historically this form of recognition was considered an employee benefit or entitlement, e.g. you stay with us for a certain amount of time and you're entitled to receive something from us, often a token gift like a watch to symbolize the concept of time.

But as you know, times have changed, both in how long (or short) people are staying at companies, but also in how organizations are realizing the importance of ongoing and continuous appreciation, doing so in a more inclusive manner. More and more companies are coming to see the benefits of a modern approach to years of service, which is to celebrate your work anniversaries more frequently to show appreciation for contributions, foster a sense of belonging and connect people to the organization.

This change was evident in the survey that I conducted for this book, which showed a shift from what was common in the past, which was to recognize employees every 10 years or so, to more frequent recognition. According to the companies saying they recognize years of service, this is how often they do so:

- 47% recognize every five years
- 30% recognize every year
- 13% recognize every 10 years
- 4% recognize every three years and then every five years
- 3% recognize after 20 or 25 years

Rebel challenge – reduce the timing

My challenge to you in this section is the same as the last section, which is to reduce the time between when you recognize and celebrate years of service. Ask yourself, what would happen if we did it every year? You don't need to spend money to do this, it could be an e-card, an email, a call from your boss or something to acknowledge and show appreciation for you being with the company for another year. You probably do it already for birthdays, so why not anniversaries?!

Besides a change in timing, another change that I've seen over the years is in what companies are doing to recognize years of service. Gone are the carriage clocks and watches, thank goodness, with companies introducing more flexibility and creativity. In respect to flexibility, according to my survey, around 58% of companies are presenting employees with gift cards, vouchers or cash, giving them the choice to decide what is right for them.

Regarding creativity, we're seeing many companies think outside of the box when it comes to these awards as well. One example is Atlassian, who for 10 years has a personalized bobblehead that is created and presented to the employee. Another example is Zappos, where they have personalized license plates created beginning at year one, which change in color every five years.

At Venables Bell & Partners, they recognize years of service with their "boot award," which is given at five years of service. Employees receive two things: a life-sized glass boot and $1,000. The catch, and what makes this different from traditional approaches to years of service, is that the money is not for the individual; it's to be used for others in the company. Whether it's picking up the tab at a local bar, taking team members out for a bit of 1:1 coaching or pooling award money to take a group out for a meal, the intent is to use it for others. "It's a way for the veterans to share what they know, carry on the culture and build relationships across the company. It creates cross-pollination, sharing with the wide-eyed and hungry youngsters what it takes to succeed," says Paul Venables, founder and CEO.

Determining recognition budgets

Let me end this section by addressing the "elephant in the room," which is your recognition budget. I say this because like the phrase, which talks about a topic that is enormous, controversial and makes us all feel uncomfortable, so too are recognition budgets. And that's because regardless of whether your company is big or small, the industry you work in or the country where you operate, we all struggle with figuring out what amounts to use for our individual recognition rewards and what overall recognition budget we should have.

My approach to answering these two questions is slightly different than others, as I start in a different place. Instead of starting by asking "how much do we have in our recognition budget," I start by asking "how do we want our people to feel through recognition"? For as I said in the Introduction, for appreciation to genuinely happen, it all needs to start with a feeling.

4 steps for developing recognition budgets

Once you've answered these questions, here are the four steps I follow to develop a recognition budget. To illustrate it, I've created an example of a service company having 100 employees and a recognition pyramid with the three levels as well as a years of service plan, and where money is given as points to spend on a recognition platform:

Step One: Determine the individual recognition plan rewards. This first step is where you figure out exactly which rewards you will give under each individual recognition plan. Keeping in mind the nine tips shared in the previous section, this is where I suggest you brainstorm with your project team to come up with the feeling, and thus the reward(s), to give for each plan.

- At the **everyday level,** we wanted our employees to feel appreciated for their help and contributions. We decided that an e-card would do this best, so no financial cost for rewards at this level.

- At the **above and beyond level**, we wanted to again show appreciation, but we also wanted employees to feel special by giving them a reward to recognize their efforts and impact. At this level we had two different plans, both of which could be given at any point in time – the first was one given by peers and was a small step from the entry-level recognition in terms of the impact of their actions, and the second was given by managers and was a bigger step in terms of the impact it had on the company.

  We asked ourselves, what would we give this person to create the feeling linked to their contributions if we were buying it ourselves? For the first plan, we decided it would be something like a nice bottle of wine, a box of chocolates or a bouquet of flowers. For this reason, the financial value of this award was $15. For the second plan, we looked at two things – first, what would we want to give them to create the associated feeling, deciding on something like lunch for two at a moderately-priced restaurant, and second, the relativity and step up from the first award. For these reasons, the financial value of this award was $30, which was twice the value of the previous award.

- At the **best of the best level**, which was our recognition plan where employees nominated one another each quarter to win individual and team-based awards, we again wanted employees being recognized to feel appreciated and special for their higher level of contributions.

  We went back to thinking about the feeling we wanted to create with the reward and decided it would be something like a dinner for two with a bottle of wine at a moderately-priced restaurant, looking at it within the context of the other awards to ensure it was a step up from the awards in the middle level. For these reasons, the financial value of this award was $60, which was twice the value of the previous award.

- For **years of service recognition**, we wanted all of our employees to feel appreciated for their contributions each and every year. For this reason, every year employees receive an e-card, which has no financial value. In addition, to celebrate key service milestones we also give employees an extra day off which they can use during their anniversary year as a way to thank them for their time. There is no financial value for this award to the employee, but for jobs that are customer-facing, we needed to budget for the cost of covering the employee's shift.

Step Two: Estimate the number of recipients.
The next step is to estimate how many recipients you believe there will be for each of your individual recognition plans.

- At the **everyday recognition level**, the e-cards, there is no cost, so there is no need to estimate the number of recipients for the budgeting process. However, I still estimate this so that I can measure the overall success of the program against how many employees are receiving recognition.

- At the **above and beyond level**, for the $15 reward, we estimated that every employee would receive three of these rewards for the year. We did this because the jump from the entry to the middle level was not that too big, and thus we felt that all employees would be able to contribute at this level throughout the year. For the $30 reward, we estimated that 35% of our employees, roughly one-third, would receive one of these rewards for the year based on the step up from the previous level of recognition.

- At the **best of the best level**, the $60 reward, we knew that five employees would receive this award each quarter as well as one team. For the team, we gave them $250 to spend on a team-based activity.

- For **years of service**, we estimated the average cost of covering a shift to be $200. Based on reviewing tenure data, we found that 10 employees would receive the extra day off, and of them, half were in service jobs and thus their replacement costs would need to be put into the recognition budget.

Step Three: Calculate your initial budget.

Then next step is to calculate your budget for your employees using the numbers from steps one and two.

Pyramid level	Reward Amount	Calculations	Budget
Level 1	0	0	$0
Level 2	$15	3 rewards/employee @ $15/award for 100 employees	$4,500
Level 2	$30	35% of 100 employees = 35 employees @ $30/reward	$1,050
Level 3	$60	5 employees/quarter for individual rewards = 20 employees @ $60/reward 1 team/quarter = 4 teams @ $250/reward	$2,200
Years of service	$200*	5 employees @ $200 to cover the cost of their	$1,000
Total:			**$8,750**

* This represents the cost of covering the employee's shift on their extra day off.

Step Four: Calculate your final budget.

To finalize your budget, taking it from step three to a final number, I'd suggest considering the following:

- **Marketing fees** – You may have fees associated with marketing your recognition plan, e.g. posters, flyers, prizes,

etc., so determine what these are and add these to your
budget.

- **Administration fees** – Depending on what you decide to
  do, you may have administration fees to cover the cost of
  your recognition platform, or if you do it in-house, the cost
  of maintaining your program (which includes people's time!).
  Determine these and add these to your budget.

- **Rounding** – Finally, when it comes to your initial budget,
  I'd suggest rounding your budget up. You'll want to do this
  for at least the first year, as your estimates may not be 100%
  correct, and you want to make sure you have enough in your
  budget to cover all of your recognition moments.

How others are budgeting recognition

It's always good to see what others are doing, so let's have a look at
what other companies are spending on recognition rewards. As always,
use this as a reference, starting by developing what you think are the
right rewards and right budget for your company and your workforce.

- According to a study by WorldatWork[39], almost 50% of
  companies budget between 0.1% to 0.3% of their payroll
  budget for recognition.

- According to the 2020 State of Recognition Report, more than
  half of organizations spend less than $100 per employee per
  year on recognition. Here is how they break it down:

  - 25% allocate $1 - 50/year
  - 36% allocate $51 - 100/year
  - 20% allocate $101 - 200/year
  - 7% allocate $201 - 400/year
  - 12% allocate $400+/year

---

39   2019 "Trends in Employee Recognition" report by WorldatWork and Maritz Motivation.

Spend by recognition pyramid levels

As mentioned earlier, survey data such as that shown above amalgamates all of the recognition plans into one number. So to provide you with more specific data, in the survey[40] I conducted for this book, I asked participants to share their spend for each of the primary levels of the recognition pyramid. Here are the results from companies reporting this information:

- **Everyday recognition** – 31% give awards valued up to $25, 29% valued $26 - $50, 17% valued $51 - $100, and 14% valued $101 and more.

- **Above and beyond recognition** – 31% give awards valued up to $101 and more, 25% valued $26 - $50, 18% valued $51 - $100, and 17% valued up to $25.

- **Best of the best recognition** – 71% give awards valued up to $101 and more, 12% valued $51 - $100, 8% valued $26 - $50, and 1% valued up to $25.

Rebel challenge – make sure you spend your budget wisely

My challenge to you is to look at where your recognition budget is being spent and make sure that it's being spent in the most meaningful and effective ways. For example, is 90% of it being spent on 5% of your population? If so, you probably have 95% of your workforce feeling unappreciated as you only have 10% of your budget left over to spend on recognition for them. If you genuinely want to achieve your objectives you need to make sure that your money, your budget, is focused and spent in the right ways.

---

40 To download a free copy of the full survey results, go to www.debcohr.com/free-resources

5 – Decide how your recognition plans will work

The next question to answer is the "how" – how will you ensure that your recognition program and individual recognition plans deliver on your objectives once they're in place? I want to stress that this is just as important as designing the "right" recognition program, for I've seen fantastic ones fail if this isn't done well.

During this step, I'll address these four topics:

1. **Manage** – how will you manage and operationalize your recognition plan?

2. **Communicate** – how will you communicate your recognition plans to ensure your employees engage with them?

3. **Train** – how will you train your workforce to ensure they understand and engage with recognition?

4. **Measure** – how will you measure your recognition programs to understand if/how they are meeting your objectives?

Manage

Let's start with how you'll manage your new recognition plans, which I highly encourage you to address **at the same time** as when you're designing them. That way, you can ensure you manage your program in a way that meets your objectives when you're ready to launch.

There are two ways to manage your programs, manually or through a technology platform. I've done it both ways, but my preference is the latter, as it can deliver recognition in a more seamless, flexible and global way. Here's how technology can help you meet these three objectives:

- **Seamless** – One of the biggest reasons I've seen recognition plans fail is because it's not easy – not easy to give recognition, not easy to receive recognition, and not easy to participate in the recognition given to others. By making the recognition experience smooth and continuous, you remove hurdles that prevent disengagement with your recognition programs.

- **Flexible** – Another challenge I've seen with recognition plans is that they aren't flexible enough to meet a company's needs. It's important to build flexibility into the management approach and processes so that if your recognition program needs to change what and how things are done, you'll be able to do so with little hassle and effort. A perfect example of this has been with the COVID-19 pandemic, with companies quickly adding e-cards to show appreciation in different ways during these challenging times.

- **Global** – And finally, you want to be able to manage your programs in a global way, whether this means you are in multiple countries or multiple locations within one country. It's all about making things easy, especially for every employee regardless of where they are to have access to the system and, when it comes to reward-based programs, have access to rewards that are relevant and meaningful to them.

In addition, by harnessing the power of recognition technology I've seen these other four benefits:

- **Creates a strong brand** – helps create and showcase strong brands to create interest and engagement with our recognition programs.

- **Delivers recognition in a more timely way** – makes it almost immediate to send and receive recognition from wherever our employees are, whether that's on a laptop computer, home office or on their cell phone when they are out and about.

- **Delivers an end-to-end experience** – creates a seamless and impactful end-to-end experience that drives engagement and a feeling of being appreciated.

- **Creates social engagement** – lets employees recognize others in the same way they do in their personal life through social media, with others being able to jump into the recognition conversation with likes, hearts and countless other emojis.

Communicate

If your company truly wants to harness the power of recognition to achieve your objectives, you must communicate it in a way that informs, engages, and appeals to their personal and emotional needs. By doing this you'll meet the objectives of communication, which is to create a *shared meaning*, a *call to action* and a *return on your investment*.

The right communication tactics keep recognition top of mind for employees, reminding them what recognition is and why it is important, driving and engaging with your recognition plans over and over again. I describe this as using communication as a recognition "hook," something to grab and then keep your employee's attention. When I interviewed Reward Gateway (see play in Chapter 5), they shared how they've woven recognition into the majority of their communication messages in one way or another. Whether it's the CEO thanking people during one of his weekly business update blogs, or a team sharing product updates that include naming those responsible for these successes, they intentionally make recognition front and center when communicating to their people. And to make it easy to connect the two, when names are mentioned in their digital communication platform, there is a direct link to where they can recognize the colleague through their digital recognition platform.

As you develop your communications strategy and messages to share information on your recognition program, here are some things to keep in mind. These guidelines go beyond recognition programs, so hopefully they will help you in a variety of ways as you communicate with your people:

- **Be open, honest and transparent**
  The absolute starting point and the absolute key to effective communication is to be open, honest and transparent.

Without this, you create mistrust and disengagement, and you fuel fear and uncertainty. So start and end with the truth, giving your employees enough information to feel in the know, bringing them into your circle of trust and helping you and them survive in these challenging times.

- **Keep your messages short**
  Let's face it, our employees don't have much of an attention span when it comes to communications. In fact, I read an article that said that the average human attention span has reduced from 12 seconds to eight seconds over the years. It's important to understand and respect this by communicating in a short and straightforward way. Challenge yourself with every word and every sentence, asking yourself if they are really necessary, or if it will just lose the precious attention of your workforce. Focus on giving your employees exactly and entirely what they need, in as few words as possible.

- **Repeat key messages**
  Another communications challenge is retention, for according to the "forgetting curve," on average we forget 50% of the information in an hour, 70% in 24 hours and 90% in a week. One way to overcome these odds is to repeat your key messages, ensuring that some, if not all of them, will stick.

- **Share stories**
  Another way to overcome the retention challenge is through storytelling, sharing recognition stories to make your communications engaging and create interest. It not only draws people into the message, but it also creates something that will bring your key messages to life in a way that a bunch of bullets on a page will never do. By the way, that's why half of my book is stories, helping the concepts I write about come to life and jump off the pages.

At Nationwide (see play in Chapter 5) they developed a unique and innovative communications campaign to drive awareness and engagement with their new online recognition platform. Here are four examples of what was included in the campaign:

- **Webcast** – It began with a webcast involving their CEO, Chief People Officer, and one of their annual recognition award winners talking about what recognition meant to them, sharing their favorite recognition stories, and ending with them talking about what they liked about the new platform. This format intentionally focused on the "why" and not the "what," drawing employees into the feelings associated with recognition, and not just the actions required.

- **Radio program** – These personal stories continued throughout the first month of the launch with employees sharing them on the Nationwide radio program, talking again about the power of recognition and the difference it had made to them.

- **Recognition poem** – Next came the creation of a recognition poem, which aligns with Nationwide's long-running business poetry campaign series called "Voices," and was written as a way to thank everyone for recognizing each other during a challenging year and to encourage people to do more of it going forward. The response to it was incredible, with employees sharing it across their network and proving their meaningful connection to the poem.

Here's an excerpt from the poem, that was written by Nationwide employee Erin Bolens:

> *There's no limit to how many people's days you can make –*
> *Two, four, six, eight? Tell us, who do you appreciate?*
> *Or rather tell them,*
> *make someone feel great*
> *by saying they've made you feel great –*
> *too good an opportunity not to take.*

In addition to the poem, they also ran a special launch competition, with the person engaging the most with the platform winning a recognition poem that was written just for them. The winner of the competition was an employee who had a poem written for their mother, someone they had not seen during the pandemic, but who they wanted to thank and recognize.

Train

As with communication, if you do not train your workforce on recognition, you are setting your recognition program up for failure. It's like giving someone a new car and saying "drive it" without explaining to them how to do this (which by the way is exactly what happened to me when I bought my first gear shift car, and it was not only scary but dangerous for me and others!). By training your managers and employees, it helps them understand the importance of recognition, e.g. why you're putting it in place, how to use it and their responsibilities.

Companies can train their workforce in a variety of ways, from formal to informal training, face-to-face sessions to online tutorials, to manuals, "how-to" guides, to anything and everything in between. As you develop your approach, consider the key times when training should take place, such as when an employee joins the company, or when they become a manager for the first time, and create training that will meet their needs and support them to assume their role for recognition at your company. Here are a few examples taken from plays appearing in Chapter 5:

- At the University of Lincoln, they take case studies from their annual recognition awards and weave them into their onboarding process to show what good looks like and to highlight how recognition is done. This educates, informs and inspires employees from the start of their career at the University.

- At Shell Energy, they created a how-to guide to help employees understand what their recognition program was all about and how it worked. They house it on their recognition platform, using it as an integral part of their communication and training strategy.

Measure

And finally, a key part of your "how" is how you measure the performance and impact of your recognition program through key metrics such as return on investment (ROI), retention, employee engagement, productivity, turnover, etc. It's important to collect data on these metrics regularly to show if and how the program has been a success or failure against your recognition objectives.

Here are some examples of what is commonly measured and reported on:

- **Usage** – This measures interaction with the program and individual plans. It could include the number of recognitions sent, the number of award nominations made, the number of clicks on recognition stories, etc.

- **Social activity** – If you have an online recognition platform, this also measures interaction with the program and plans but is specific to social interaction. It could include the number of likes or comments employees are receiving or giving.

- **Engagement survey** – Often employee engagement surveys ask the question – "Do you feel recognized and appreciated for your efforts?" This is a great measure to keep track of, understanding specifically whether your recognition program is helping to improve a feeling of appreciation.

- **HR metrics** – Review data from other HR metrics such as turnover and attraction to see if recognition has had an impact on them. Whether that's with changes in the actual numbers, e.g. a decrease in turnover, or online reviews by employees that have helped with attraction, review and connect the dots between your other metrics and your recognition initiatives.

- **Anecdotes** – And finally, don't underestimate the power of a great story, sharing specific stories and examples that highlight the value your program and plans are having with your workforce. These demonstrate the value of investment (VOI), as you won't have a hard measurement.

Another important reason for measuring your recognition program performance is to help you understand areas and opportunities for improvement. For example, does one department or location consistently not recognize one another, does one manager recognize certain teams over others, is there one company value that is never recognized against? There may be reasons for all of these things happening, but without measuring and then analyzing the data, you'll never know whether it's fine or it's a problem that needs to be overcome.

6 – Design your recognition branding

The final decisions you'll need to make relate to the branding of your recognition program, which includes the names and designs. Although this isn't absolutely necessary, I've found it to be extremely helpful in making that all-important first impression with your employees, making them decide in an instant whether they'll engage with your recognition program or not. I actually love working on this step, as it's where you give your hard work a meaningful and often fun personality.

Naming your program

One of the most important decisions you will make is the name of your recognition program and the individual recognition plans. The name will determine your overall brand and theme, and, of course, this is the name your employees will use over and over again as they engage with them. For this reason, I'd suggest starting to think about your names as soon as you develop your recognition plans. In fact, I often try out names in the middle of the design process, as I find it helps me test out whether it will work when I eventually roll it out.

> **When you name your program, go back to the concept of a "feeling," and come up with ones that deliver the right feeling for the right actions and behaviors.**

Here are a few tips I've picked up over the years from working with some wonderful people in marketing to make sure your names will lead you to success:

- **Create meaning** – the name should create meaning, relating back to the plan and the intent of it, doing so as quickly and effortlessly as possible. This goes for the overall recognition program name as well as the individual plans, as they can create meaning to show the difference between the plans and the levels. Here are some examples:

- At Burton's Biscuit Company, all of their names relate to their business, which is biscuits (cookies). The program is called Bake My Day, and the individual recognition plans are: Treat Award, Crumbs Up Award, and the Smart Cookie Award

- At LinkedIn, all of their individual recognition plan names align with a theme and show an increasing importance and impact of each as follows: Shout Out, Cheers, Applause, Limelight, Spotlight, Ovation, Rave, and Encore.

- At Reward Gateway, their program is called Appreci8 to clearly state its purpose and reflect the eight values they recognize against. Their individual plans names also state their purpose and intent as follows: High Five, You Rock and Game Changer.

- **Keep the name simple** – the name should be easy to understand, pronounce and remember. Keep in mind that not all words mean the same thing in all places, so this is especially important if you have a global and/or diverse workforce.

- **Acronyms** – one approach to naming your program is with an acronym, which can make it fun and easy to remember, and if done well, can create an additional layer of meaning. Here are some examples:

  - STAR, which stands for "Special Thanks and Recognition"
  - LOVE, which stands for "Living Our Values Every day"
  - RED, which stands for "Recognizing Excellence Daily"

- **Think beyond the now** – Finally, it's important to select names that can stand the test of time and be more evergreen. You don't want to be changing them over and over again, as it could confuse and disengage your people.

I suggest that when you develop your names, you involve your employees to help you do this. It not only creates a sense of ownership, but "my" best names have come from my workforce. Here are some examples of some of the names I've either used or have seen to help inspire you if you're looking for a name for your recognition program:

- Above & beyond
- Accolate
- AllStars
- Applause
- Cheers
- Inspire
- Kudos
- Shine
- Simply Thanks
- Stand Out
- Star
- The Extra Mile

Creating your designs

As they say, a picture is worth a thousand words. This is absolutely true when it comes to your recognition designs, as they can say and mean things that your words alone can't convey. When done well, the images create excitement, association and engagement, bringing to life the intent and meaning of your recognition programs and plans.

Here are a few tips I've picked up over the years from designers that I hope will help you as well:

- **Be eye-catching** – It's important to create images that will attract the attention of your employees, with them yearning to engage with them so they can see what's behind them.

- **Keep it simple** – Creating an image doesn't have to be complicated, in fact, if you make it simple and clean it will have a much better chance of being recognized and understood at a glance. This is especially important if you have an online recognition platform, as many of your employees will be engaging with your program on their cell phones, so you want something that works well when it appears on their small screen.

- **Be meaningful and literal** – As with the name of your program and plans, the images you create need to also be meaningful and literal so that your workforce knows exactly what they mean, with no additional thought or effort going into it.

- **Be timeless** – If like the names you select, you want your images to stand the test of time, it's important to design ones that are not too gimmicky or trendy but are firmly rooted in meaning and the story you are trying to tell through them.

- **Be cohesive** – Just as your recognition plans work together, so should your images. They should work together to tell a piece of the same story, and while this doesn't mean that they all have to look exactly the same, they should fit together like pieces of a puzzle to form a complete picture.

  For example, at Homeserve their recognition program is called STAR, and all of the names of the recognition plans are themed around stars. For this reason, the images they designed have a consistent look and feel so that employees can easily recognize them as part of their recognition program.

One final tip for when you design your branding, both with the name and imagery, is to test them out with your workforce before you finalize anything. This helps ensure your program will land well with your employees, delivering the punch and impact that is required to use them as effective tools for helping you achieve your recognition objectives.

Calls to Action:

List out your recognition objectives and principles and assess whether they are the right ones to meet the needs of your business and people. If you don't have them yet, here's an opportunity to create them.

Objectives:

Principles:

Map out your recognition pyramid below, and assess whether it has the right number of levels to meet your objectives.

Evaluate the "what," "who" and "when" for each of your individual recognition plans, listing any changes that need to be made.

Doing well now:

Opportunities to improve:

Evaluate how you currently run your recognition program and individual plans (e.g. manage, communicate and train), listing any opportunities you have to do it better:

Doing well now:

Opportunities to improve:

Evaluate how you currently brand your recognition program and individual plans, listing any opportunities you have to do it better:

Doing well now:

Opportunities to improve:

Chapter 4: Maintaining your recognition program

Chapter objectives

In this chapter, we'll cover:

- The importance of giving your recognition program constant care and attention to keep it going strong to meet your recognition objectives.

- The role of your recognition "gardeners" and how you can use them to support and drive recognition at your company.

- The informal recognition tools you have to help you drive recognition and create a recognition culture.

- The approaches you can use to maintain your recognition program.

Introduction

The ancient pyramids of Egypt have been standing for centuries, withstanding the test of time through the exceptional techniques and materials used to build them. But when it comes to recognition pyramids, unfortunately, they don't have this longevity, for no matter how we build them, they require attention, maintenance, and constant care to help them survive and thrive. To further explain this let me move from pyramids to gardens, sharing a story of what happened to me.

A few years ago I broke my ankle at the start of the summer, right after I had spent a few solid weekends preparing the soil and planting the small plants that had been grown from seeds over the dark winter months. These plants had been carefully selected, nurtured, and had been part of a plan that would deliver a garden full of lovely flowers and vegetables to enjoy throughout the summer. But because of my injury, I wasn't able to tend my garden, and the beds quickly filled with weeds, with many of the plants not even surviving.

I share this story with you to emphasize and bring to life the point that a recognition program, like a garden, left unattended will not flourish, and thus will not help you achieve your recognition objectives. You need to put as much, if not more, effort into "tending" to it, doing so using a variety of techniques and approaches.

In this chapter we'll cover these, giving you what you need to keep your recognition pyramid and program strong. From the people who need to be involved to the tools you'll use, to the processes you'll follow to drive and maintain it, I'll share tips and stories to help you enhance the visibility and effectiveness of your recognition program to drive engagement, and create a strong and flourishing recognition culture.

Recognition "gardeners"

Let's start by looking at the people you need to keep your recognition program going, your advocates. Or going back to the garden analogy, your "gardeners." These are the people who help you tend to your programs in a variety of ways – from "watering" it by using it over and over again to "weeding" it by highlighting and removing obstacles that get in the way of its usage.

Leading from the top

Your first group of "gardeners" are your leaders and managers, who I'd deem your head gardeners due to the critical role they have in driving your company culture and employee engagement. And when it comes to recognition, they're absolutely key in role-modeling recognition to the rest of the workforce, showing them that it's worthy of their time and attention, and how to do it in the most meaningful and effective ways.

As shown in the data below, recognition from leaders and managers has been proven to have an impact on business results, recognition results, and even the relationship and trust between them and their teams:

- **Stronger business results:** When senior leaders are actively involved in employee recognition, companies are 9 times more likely to have strong business results[41].

- **More likely to recognize others:** When a manager recognizes their direct report, they are 2.5 more likely to recognize others[42].

- **Improved relationship with manager:** 58% of employees report that their relationship with their manager would improve with more recognition[43].

- **Improved trust:** Employees who were recognized were 34% more likely to trust senior leaders and 33% more likely to trust managers, compared to those who had never been recognized[44].

Employees work harder if managers show appreciation

Researchers at the Wharton School at the University of Pennsylvania randomly divided university fundraisers into two groups to conduct a study[45]. One group made phone calls to solicit alumni donations in the same way they always had, and the second group, who worked on a different day, received a pep talk from their director, telling them that she was grateful for their efforts. During the following week, the group who had heard her message of gratitude made 50% more fundraising calls than those who did not.

For this reason, it's critical to get your leaders and managers on board early and often, explaining to them the role they have, giving them the tools to be successful, and then holding them accountable. Here are five ideas to incorporate into the recognition training you give to your leaders and managers:

---

41 Lin, Connie. Some Big Tech Companies May be Tapping the Brakes on the Work-from-Home-Forever Trend. Fast Company.

42 Achiever's 2020 State of Recognition report.

43 Achiever's 2020 State of Recognition report.

44 Achiever's 2020 State of Recognition report.

45 Study conducted by Adam Grant and Francesca Gino 2010.

1. **Explain the importance of recognition**: The starting point for this group is to explain the "why," so why is recognition important, helping them understand why it's something they should pay attention to and put effort into. They're busy people, and if you don't start with this, and if you don't do it in a compelling and business-focused way, you'll never get them onboard. So use the data from throughout this book and create that powerful one slide that will show them without a shadow of a doubt that recognition can and will make a difference at your company.

   Just as important as sharing the reasons at a high level, is to share the reasons at a more micro level, explaining how it can benefit them and the work they are responsible for. Point out that if they want to see more of an action or behavior, they need to recognize it, sending the message that what they've done is valued and should be continued. Help them understand this, and the light bulbs will go off when it comes to their understanding and appreciation of recognition.

2. **Convert the non-believers**: Once you've explained the why, trust me, you'll still have the non-believers. You know them, they're the ones who roll their eyes as you talk about recognition and/or sit with their arms crossed to make it perfectly clear that they don't believe and don't care. We all have them, and we can't ignore them, for they not only impact their group by not role modeling recognition, but they also can convert others to non-believers based on their influence.

   For non-believers you again need to address the "why," but this time it's *their* "why." For example, are they a non-believer because they personally don't like to be recognized, so they assume it's the same for everyone else? Is it because they don't feel comfortable giving recognition? Or is it because they don't think they have time for it? By understanding their reasons you can then address and overcome them.

3. **Explain your programs**: The next thing to explain to your leaders and managers is the "what" – what are your recognition programs and how do they differ from one to

another? and "how" – how should they be used? They need to be crystal clear on this for two reasons. First, because if they use the programs in the wrong way it will have the wrong impact. Second, because as role models, if they do it wrong, then others will follow. This is so important that when I deliver my training sessions with leaders and managers I do practical exercises where we share recognition stories (e.g. what did someone do that should be recognized) and discuss as a group the best way to recognize within the company's program and plans.

4. **Create habits**: Another key point to get across to leaders and managers is the concept of making recognition a habit, creating rituals so that over time it becomes a habit. We all know that something new doesn't just happen, you need to put time and effort into it so that it happens without thinking about it.

   Here are five steps I often follow when trying to turn something into a habit. To bring it to life, I've included an example here. Keep in mind that it's just an example, and there are many other ways to turn recognition into a habit.

   - **Step 1 – Understand it:** Remind yourself why it is important.
     For example, I remind myself that recognition helps my employees feel appreciated and valued, which is good for them, me and the company.

   - **Step 2 – Goal it**: Set yourself goals to achieve.
     For this, I set a goal to spend 15 minutes twice a week to focus on recognition.

   - **Step 3 – Schedule it:** Set aside time to do this.
     To help, I lock 15 minutes in my calendar every Wednesday and Friday to do this.

   - **Step 4 – Remove it:** Remove any obstacles that could get in your way.
     For example, I make sure that I fully understand how my

company's recognition program works so that's easy to do. Also, during the week, I jot down any moments that I'll want to remember to recognize, again making it easier to do.

In Shawn Achor's book *The Happiness Advantage*, he shows that by removing the barriers that stop us from establishing a positive habit, that in just one-third of a minute we can change our life.

- **Step 5 – Assess it:** Set aside time to review and assess the differences made.
  For example, at the end of the month, I'll look at the impact my recognition has made, e.g. reactions of my employees, impact on their work.

A lovely story shared with me that illustrates a recognition ritual is of a leader who would put 10 pennies in his pocket, and every time he recognized someone he would move a penny from one pocket to another. This was a simple reminder to him to recognize people, keeping track of it in a very unique and effective way.

Let me end this by reiterating that there are many ways to create rituals and habits. The important point and action to take is to encourage your leaders and managers to find ways to do it in their own way so that recognition becomes a part of their muscle memory, something that happens without them even thinking about it. When this happens, this is when the magic of recognition takes place!

It takes more than 28 days to form a habit

You may have heard of something called the "28 day rule," which says that it takes from 21 to 28 days to create a new habit. I'm sorry to say, but according to a study by the University College London psychologist Phillippa Lally and her colleagues, this isn't true.

They found that on average the subjects in their study who were trying to learn new habits such as eating fruit daily or going jogging took 66 days before reporting that the behavior had become a habit. However, the good news is that the same study found that when forming a new habit, missing a day made no difference, so at least that myth isn't true.

Bottom line, forming a habit takes time and effort, but when it comes to recognition, it's well worth it!

---

5. **Hold them accountable** – Last but not least, once you've given your leaders and managers everything they need to be successful, it's time to hold them accountable. They need to know that recognition is an expectation of them, and that they will be held accountable. So track recognition actions against each leader and manager, and take action should you find that it doesn't meet the expectations that you set. Whether it's based on a certain number of recognitions given over a set period of time, scores from engagement surveys, or a variety of other factors, the key is to determine what you'll hold them accountable for, let them know, and then take action to ensure it's happening.

Champions of recognition

Your next group of "gardeners" are what many call their recognition champions, who, like your leaders and managers, are advocates of recognition to help drive a culture of recognition at your company. Time and time again I've seen this group of employees create awareness, excitement and engagement with my recognition programs in ways that I could never do. This is because they're on the ground and know what will and won't work, and because they're working alongside their colleagues and have the trust and attention of them that I could never have. And for this reason, I truly value and leverage all that they have to offer to help my recognition program be a success.

Recognition champions are your "passionate influencers" – people who can make recognition happen on the floor and in the hearts and minds of your workforce.

Here are two examples of companies who use champions, with their full stories appearing in Chapter 5:

- **Heineken** – At Heineken, each of their U.K. sites has a recognition champion who is responsible for owning and driving recognition. This includes working with local management to review and approve awards, ensuring all employees are aware of the program, and proactively managing recognition so that all employees are treated in a fair and consistent way.

- **Zoom** – At Zoom, they have what they call their "Happy Crew" who are not only responsible for driving recognition but owning it. This volunteer team of 200 employees from around the world work together to ensure that they have the right programs and practices in place so that all employees feel recognized by the company, their manager and their teammates.

Here are a few things to keep in mind when it comes to recognition champions:

- **Think about the selection process.**
  There is no right or wrong way to select your recognition champions. Some companies ask for volunteers, others select those that have shown that they engage with recognition at a high level. Whatever you decide, here are a few traits to ask or look for in them:

  - They have a passion for recognition, understanding the impact it can have.
  - They are committed to being a change agent, using their influencing skills to drive recognition.

- They should be strong communicators, being able to freely share information and be comfortable answering questions and collecting feedback.
- They should be knowledgeable of your recognition program and how they work. And although they don't need to be experts, they need to be willing to seek out and learn information if they don't know it.

- **Be clear about expectations.**
  Both during the selection process and throughout their time as recognition champions, it's important to be clear on what you expect of your champions. Spell out their responsibilities, helping to set them up to succeed in this important role. Here are a few sample responsibilities that you can start with if you don't have them listed already:

  - Endorse and act as a role model for recognition.
  - Feedback on things that are working well and not working well.
  - Generate ideas to make recognition real every day.
  - Share best practices with other champions.

- **Provide training and support.**
  Equally important in helping your champions succeed is to provide them with the training and support they need in this role. If you just throw them in, which I have seen done, it's a waste of their time and energy, and you won't accomplish what you need to.

  Many companies I've worked at or have supported, hold an annual event where they bring their champions together to provide ongoing training and support, as well as discuss how recognition is being used by their colleagues. This is great for their development, to brainstorm new ideas, and, just as important, to thank and recognize them for their contributions.

Recognition as a team sport

Your final group of "gardeners" you need to help you "tend" your recognition garden and help it flourish are the remainder of your workforce. And that's because, as I often explain, recognition is a team sport, where you need everyone involved and "playing" for it to work.

Think of it like a sports team, let's say basketball. If you only have the captain (the leader) playing the game, you have no chance at all of winning. You need everyone dribbling, passing and shooting the ball if you're going to defend your goal (retain your people), score (make your people feel appreciated) and win (drive business results).

In Mike Robbins book *Bring Your Whole Self to Work*, he talks about this concept of shared and team responsibility for appreciation, saying that "Focusing on and expressing appreciation for one another is a powerful way to demonstrate that we care about the people on our team. It's also necessary to our ability to challenge those around us in a healthy and productive way."

A key reason for making recognition a team sport is that you have more people looking out for recognition moments, being able to capture all the actions and behaviors that deserve appreciation. Taking it one step further, it's important to have everyone looking for recognition in all directions. Going back to basketball, it's about constantly looking forward, sidewards and even backward to see who you can pass the ball to (recognize).

> According to research by Deloitte[46], over half of the companies surveyed (53%) said that a shift to a team-based model significantly improved their performance, and 21% reported some improvement in performance. And although the research looked at the impact in respect to organizational design, it also applies to a team-based approach to recognition, with everyone getting involved and driving the effectiveness and performance of recognition.

---

46   Deloitte's 2017 Global Human Capital Trends survey.

As with your leaders and managers, it's important to educate and train your workforce in the areas mentioned in the previous section. This ensures that they're clear on the important role they have to play on your team and at your company, and they know how to recognize in the most meaningful and effective way.

Informal recognition tools

It's great to have a team of gardeners, but they'll never succeed if they don't have the right tools to help them do their job. In the last chapter we spoke about a recognition pyramid, which is your formal recognition tool, but in order to create a culture where everyone feels appreciated and recognized, you cannot rely just on this. Going back to gardening, it's like using one tool, say a rake, to do all of your gardening tasks – it just doesn't work. You need a variety of gardening tools to meet the needs of the task, and when it comes to recognition, you need a variety of recognition tools to create and drive a flourishing recognition culture to achieve your objectives.

By having multiple recognition tools, you recognize your people based on their individual contributions and individual preferences. This helps connect and recognize your people in more meaningful and lasting ways.

In this section, we'll explore some of the informal recognition tools that companies use. As you look through them, keep in mind that this is just a sampling, for I could fill an entire book with all the wonderful things that companies do. As you and your workforce select your informal recognition tools, keep in mind and match them to the following:

1. **The action and behavior** – As with the recognition pyramid, where it's important to recognize at the appropriate level based on the action and behavior, the same holds true when it comes to your informal recognition tools. Take the time to consider the scope and impact of the *input*, the action and behavior, before you select the *output*, the tool you will ultimately use to deliver recognition.

2. **The person being recognized** – When it comes to informal recognition, there are so many ways to do it. In fact, one

of the first books I read on this topic is titled *1001 Ways to Reward Employees*. But with all of these options, it's even more important to make sure that you take the time to understand personal preferences, understanding how best the individual would feel appreciated and recognized.

3. **The person giving recognition** – It's just as important for the person recognizing to find a way that works for them, reflecting their personality and their style. For example, at a previous company, one of the managers was known for recognizing by giving out a bag of handmade cookies that his partner had baked. This was so personal to him, and something that in turn meant so much to those who received them, and not just because they tasted amazing!

Recognition deck of cards

At two of my previous companies, we developed a recognition-focused deck of cards. The decks contained 52 cards showing different informal recognition tools that, like a deck of cards, were sorted into suits and were separated into categories of low-, middle- and high-cost recognition. The card ideas ranged from having your manager make you a cup of coffee, to having a special parking spot for a month, to having an extra day off, to receiving a shopping voucher. It was a fun way for employees to select which recognition tool would mean the most to them to make sure the recognition programs met their personal needs.

Since there are so many different kinds of informal recognition, I've grouped them into the following five categories to create a bit of order and structure to them:

1. Growth/development opportunities
2. Gifts
3. Time
4. Activities
5. Communication

Growth/development opportunities

When respondents were asked how they preferred to be recognized for a significant accomplishment, a study[47] by Deloitte found that almost half of them (47%) would choose a new growth opportunity. This was significantly higher than a salary increase (23%), a high performance rating (21%) or even a bonus (10%), which shows the importance employees place on their growth and development.

Understanding this, many companies have a variety of growth and development opportunities as part of their informal recognition. From sending employees on formal training classes to being able to attend or present at a meeting, to being given a mentor, to shadowing their manager, they are finding ways to use this as a recognition tool, sending the message to employees that they value and appreciate them and are committed to supporting their growth and development.

An example of this is KP Snacks's Living Leadership program, which includes an immersion week working with a charity. As well as developing leadership skills, the program is used to recognize achievements, being seen as something that employees want to aspire to and be part of. "For some people, going on this program is more meaningful and more important than other forms of recognition. I can still remember when the CEO called me to invite me on it, recognizing me for both my contribution and my potential. It was a 'wow' moment in my leadership journey, the investment in me meant more than any award or bonus and the fact that the CEO took the time to make the call, I felt valued – you don't forget those moments, " says Rachel Ovington, Senior HR Leader at KP Snacks.

Gifts

This category includes a wide variety of informal recognition tools, from company-branded merchandise to food, to anything and everything in between. When it comes to gifts, I've seen companies and individuals put their own individual mark on them, coming up with ways to show appreciation in wild and wonderful ways.

---

47   The Practical Magic of Thank You study by Deloitte 2019.

Earlier I shared the example of the manager who gives out home-baked cookies, and another great example is one that was told to me by Neil Piper, Chief People Officer at KFC. He explained that many people at KFC have their own informal recognition awards that they use to bring out their character and personality through recognition. One of his is something called the "Culture Vulture" award, which is a £3.99 cuddly vulture dog toy, which he gives out to people for bringing their culture to life.

I've also seen gifts used to recognize company or project-wide achievements and contributions. For example, at one company I was known for recognizing my teams for project-related gifts to celebrate and thank everyone for being a part of the project and helping to achieve our shared results. From coffee mugs to t-shirts to sweets, I used this as a way to make everyone feel valued and appreciated for their hard work (especially for having to work with me).

Another example are gifts that are passed from one employee to another, like what we used to do back in elementary school with a prized stuffed animal. In Chapter 3, I shared the example of Radio Flyer's golden wagon that is passed from employee to employee along with a personalized note, and another example is Hoxby Collective's "Hoxby of Notes Book," which is a book that is passed from member to member along with lovely recognition notes.

Here are some other examples of company-wide recognition gifts taken from an eBook[48] I wrote during the pandemic, showing how companies cared for and recognized their employees during this challenging time:

- **Gift boxes** – Each week during the lockdown, employees at Tony's Chocoloney received special gift boxes. The first one was a QuaranTony survival kit, packed with the essentials required for lockdown including Red Bull and Jagermeister since their company ski trip was canceled due to the pandemic. Others included food from local restaurants, to put smiles on the faces of not only their employees but also the businesses they were supporting. And to close out the lockdown, the final box was a Staycation kit, packed with

---

48   For a copy of this free eBook, go to www.debcohr.com/free-resources

everything to have a beach vacation at home since travel was still not allowed, and on a more serious note, the choice of a few books on the topic of anti-racism.

- **Face masks** – At Kellogg's they had special "Tony the Tiger" face masks prepared and sent to all of their employees during the pandemic to show them that they cared for the health, wellbeing and safety of their workforce. "The reaction was phenomenal. Employees were taking selfies and sharing them all over social media! It showed us that recognition that is dropped in can be really important and impactful," says Samantha Berry-Thomas, Vice President of European Human Resources.

- **Food allowance** – Before the pandemic, only managers at Welcome Break received a food allowance to pay for their meals when they worked at one of their motorway service stations. But to show they cared about and appreciated every employee coming into work during lockdown, they extended it to them all. "We wanted everyone to have lunch on us," said Nicola Marshall, People Director.

- **Employee benefit** – Prior to the pandemic, Macmillan's Employee Assistance Program (EAP) was only available to their 2,000 permanent employees. But seeing the need to also support and show appreciation to their 20,000 volunteers, they decided to extend and provide EAP to them as well. "The pandemic really made us think of our workforce differently, making sure we met the needs of our whole team," says Dewey. Since this is not a normal practice, it really brought their value of "acting as one team" to life as it shows the personal care delivered to each and every important member of their workforce.

Time

Another popular form of informal recognition is giving time, or, more accurately, time off. I've found that time is something that's become more important and more valued based on our new ways of working. Here are a few ways to give your employees the valuable gift of time:

- **Ad hoc time off** – This is probably the most obvious and common way to informally recognize through time, which is when managers make ad hoc decisions to let individuals or teams go home early, come in late, etc. It shows the team that their manager recognizes the hard work they've been doing and that they are appreciated.

- **Office closures** – Another practice that I've seen grow in popularity over the years is to close the office early and/or for days at certain times of the year. For example, I've worked at companies that close the office at noon on a Friday during the summer so that employees can enjoy the sunshine, or close for a week in December so employees can spend time with their families during the holiday season. Whichever way and whichever practice, these small acts can have a huge impact, and as an extra bonus, can often cost you nothing!

- **Development days** – Another thing companies do is to give time off in the form of development days, which can be done either formally or informally, and fits under the categories of both time and growth/development recognition. By doing this, it signals to their employees that they appreciate them, and want to give them the time they need to learn and develop.

- **Volunteer days** – The last example, giving time off for volunteer days, can again be done formally or informally, and can again have a powerful impact on your workforce. At a previous company, I introduced three days per year for volunteer days and was surprised and delighted by the number of people who came up to thank me for doing this, saying that it showed that we valued their commitment to supporting what was important to them, giving them the time to do so.

Throughout the pandemic, we saw time being used by many companies as a way to recognize their employees for the contributions they were making and as a way to support them during challenging times. Some gave days or weeks off, while others changed their approach to their annual paid time off entitlement. An example of this is what Honest Burgers, a U.K. restaurant group, did by announcing in 2021 a special four-week paid sabbatical benefit, which is two weeks more than their usual two-week limit. When asked why they decided to do this, Oli Cavaliero, Head of Employer Brand, said, "With almost 70% of our workforce not being U.K. nationals, they were not able to travel home to visit family and friends over the last year, and have been missing out on this. We wanted to give employees this extended time to catch up with family or friends, or just take in the sights of London." So until 2023, their employees will be able to take up to four weeks of their unused holidays to do just that, recognizing these special times and showing their gratitude and appreciation for their contributions.

Activities

The next category of informal recognition tools are activities, which, as with all your informal recognition tools, will likely vary based on your company's culture. What's nice about this is the flexibility to do these activities on an individual, team or company-wide basis. Here are just a few examples:

- **Attend an external awards ceremony** – Many organizations have formal internal recognition awards ceremonies, but in addition to this, some companies use external award ceremonies as a way to thank people for their contributions to a project and/or action. I've done this myself, where I invited the project team to attend an awards ceremony event, signaling to them that regardless of whether we win or lose the award, their contributions were valued and appreciated.

- **Act as employee advocate** – Another example, which could be considered an activity or a development opportunity, was shared with me when I interviewed Abcam for their play. They told me of how they recognized one of their HR Administrators for her contributions by giving her the opportunity to be a company advocate, personally contacting every new employee before they join, and welcoming them to the company. This activity "brings her joy by doing the things she really wants to do, and at the same time makes her and the new employees feel valued and appreciated," said Nick Skinner, SVP Human Resources. After all, it's great to be known as the "face" of your company and shows how much of an example that particular employee sets.

- **Have a meal cooked by the hotel chef** – Another story shared with me was from a proud father, whose daughter was working as a housekeeper in a hotel in Scotland, and was treated to a meal cooked by the hotel's chef on Housekeeper Appreciation Day. He said that normally they were given cold food from the hotel, so this was extra special for them, especially as they wouldn't be able to afford a meal at this luxury hotel.

Here are two more examples taken from my eBook previously mentioned, showing how companies cared for and showed appreciation to their employees during the pandemic through informal recognition activities:

- **"How to have a holiday at home" webinar** – At Atos, they ran a variety of events for their workforce, including webinars and videos on how to make the most of a vacation day at home, something many were doing during the lockdown. Ideas were presented from different perspectives so that colleagues could relate and learn from them. A dedicated virtual event webinar brought ideas together ranging from a parent sharing how to have a camping day off in your backyard, to an employee living on their own who did everything virtually, from riding roller coasters to going on safari tours.

- **Kids summer camp** – At Zoom, since many employees didn't have somewhere to go for the summer because of the pandemic, they took the idea of Zoomitude, which is their word for "gratitude," and created Camp Zoomitude, bringing summer camp in-house. Both kids and parents loved that three days a week they could join in on camp-based activities as well as the Friday recap called "Smores N' More" with a family sing-a-long where they were joined by the CEO himself!

Communication

The final category of informal recognition is communication, which, going back to my gardening analogy, I like to think of as the "fertilizer" of your recognition program as it provides "nutrients" to help it flourish and grow. And just like fertilizer, by sprinkling it either on top of formal recognition or in simple informal ways, your employees will feel valued and appreciated. Here are a few ways to sprinkle communications into your programs:

- **Handwritten notes** – Many companies I've interviewed use informal and ad hoc handwritten recognition notes as a way to supplement their formal recognition program. For example, at Missguided they have what they call a "Celebration Station" set up on each floor that contains recognition postcards, and at KP Snacks, each site has a stack of "call out cards" which employees can use to write handwritten recognition notes. And although both companies have a digital recognition platform where e-cards can be sent, they both decided that they also wanted to have these as another way to informally recognize one another.

- **Shout outs** – Another effective way to communicate recognition is through something called a "shout out." In my book *Build It: The Rebel Playbook for Employee Engagement,* I shared a story about SnackNation's "Crush It Call," where every Friday at 4:00 p.m., their employees would share stories of how colleagues had "crushed it," shining a light on the accomplishments and everyday victories that might otherwise go unsung.

  Another example is what Blinkist calls "The Awesomes," which is when employees write in to share recognition stories, and then read them out during their weekly all-hands call. And because Blinkist has a team-based culture, in addition to the individual shout out, they also recognize the team behind the contributions.

  These are both great examples of shouting out recognition in an informal and yet effective way. And as an added bonus, these gestures help facilitate team bonding, break down silos and give everyone a better understanding of the business and their fellow employees.

- **Social shout outs** – Many of the digital recognition platforms automatically do social shout outs, immediately sharing recognition moments to spark involvement and visibility from your workforce. However, if you don't yet have one, another method is to do social shout outs on whatever social platform you use to communicate with your workforce (e.g. Slack). It won't do everything a digital recognition platform does, but it still sends recognition shout outs and gets people involved. My husband, who has to listen to me talk about recognition every day, put something like this in place at his company as they didn't have anything, creating animated values icons to get people involved and shout out achievements based on their values.

- **Celebration shout outs** – Another way that companies are recognizing their employees is through what I'm going to call "celebration moments." They are anything from promotions to birthdays to anniversaries to the birth of a child or buying a new house – anything and everything that you want to shout out and celebrate. This recognizes your employee's professional and personal moments to be celebrated, making them feel seen, valued and appreciated. This is something Missguided recently changed when they found out through an engagement survey that employees didn't feel fully recognized because promotions and job changes weren't being celebrated and shouted out. By making this simple change and adding to the celebration shout outs they were already doing, it improved employees' feelings of being appreciated. It's proof that small changes like this can complete the recognition cycle, creating a holistic and effective approach to recognition.

Another example is from KP Snacks, where they have a practice called "Feel Good Friday," which is a weekly email that shares the names of all Call Out recipients that were recognized, as seen on their social recognition platform. This helps add to the impact and visibility in these recognition moments, as employees can see and get involved with either (or both) the email or social recognition wall.

Recognition maintenance

This last section talks about maintenance, which in gardening involves different activities to keep your plants growing, your weeds away and even attract wildlife. In recognition, there are also important activities that need to take place to continually engage your workforce, create a recognition culture and meet your recognition objectives. These activities will differ based on the design of your recognition pyramid and your informal recognition practices, your workforce, your culture, etc., but regardless of this, you'll want to think through your maintenance and plan it out well in advance. Once a year, twice a year, every quarter, for example, it's important to come together to review and update your maintenance plan to ensure it's working in the way you need it to, adapting it as necessary. And to get you started with this, I've shared below four ways to maintain your programs.

Integrate into ways of working

For recognition to be effective it needs to naturally and organically flow, seamlessly integrating into your culture and your ways of working. Think of it like water naturally flowing down a stream, gracefully moving the water from land to sea. The same can and should be done with recognition, for if we naturally integrate it into our work practices, it will enhance its visibility, increase utilization and help us achieve our overall recognition objectives.

To achieve this integration, I like to think about it in terms of "touchpoints," which are any and every opportunity you have to bring recognition to the forefront. From making it a part of your onboarding sessions or your performance management process to giving it a starring role in your company newsletter or town hall meetings, it's important to find ways to integrate recognition into these touchpoints. Here are a few examples taken from the plays appearing later in this book:

- **Welcome e-card** – At Key Forensics, they have a special e-card designed to send to all new employees to welcome them to the company. The added benefit is that it introduces them to their digital recognition platform and sends the message from the start that recognition is a key part of their culture and ways of working.

- **Induction stories** – As part of their induction process, at the University of Lincoln they share recognition stories, highlighting what good looks like and also putting the spotlight on recognition from the start.

- **Communication practices** – At Reward Gateway they integrate recognition into their communication practices and activities. They do this in two ways, first when sharing stories on their company's internal communications platform they mention the names of people who have contributed and the accomplishments that they've made to put the spotlight on recognition. Second, using their own technology, they have a direct link from the person's (or people's!) name to their digital recognition platform, where employees can easily recognize colleagues when they read the stories. Together, they've found this to be extremely effective in driving ongoing and meaningful recognition.

  "One of the things our clients can struggle with is making recognition consistent. If it feels like it's 'one more thing to do, it is easy to let recognition fall off the plate. That's why we try to get recognition to show up wherever they are. From a technology perspective, having the ability to recognize from communications – or even from Slack – makes it that much more likely it will happen," says Alexandra Powell, Director of Client Culture and Engagement, Reward Gateway.

- **Performance management practices** – At Deloitte, they link and embed recognition into their performance management processes. For example, when a goal is met and is noted in the performance management platform, there is a link provided to take the manager or colleague directly to the recognition platform. Here, they can easily and quickly recognize one another for achieving this goal.

  "We don't want people to have to search for things, so we've tried to package it all together within the flow of work, making it easier to do the things we want our people to do. The result is a continuous and full circle performance management (and recognition) experience for our employees," says Breckon Jones, Head of Employee Experience at Deloitte.

- **Manager training** – And finally, something I've done at manager training is to have a section specifically on recognition. During this, I explain their role as a recognition role modeler, why recognition is important and how it works at the company. We then do an exercise where they practice giving recognition using postcards I bring to the training. By doing this, they not only practice giving recognition firsthand but the responsibility is integrated into their understanding of their role as a manager.

Create targeted campaigns

Another way to keep recognition flowing is through campaigns, which are targeted activities you organize to raise awareness and bring people back to recognition from time to time. By doing this it keeps recognition fresh, giving your employees a reminder of why and how to recognize, and helps create a strong recognition culture.

There are countless ways to do this, but here are a few that I've pulled from the plays appearing later in this book:

- **E-card campaigns** – At Certis Security they have a variety of e-card campaigns, sending all employees recognition e-cards to mark specific events throughout the year. A recent example was on R U OK Day, a day that encourages employees to have open and honest conversations about mental health with themselves and others, and which this past year (September 2021) was an unusually difficult time with Australians battling bushfires, floods and a global pandemic. To acknowledge the extra stressors, special "R U OK" e-cards were sent to their entire workforce to connect and encourage them during this challenging time, along with a company-wide campaign and pledge to find ways to check in and connect with each other.

Teleperformance also holds special e-card campaigns throughout the year, where they create special e-cards that employees can send to one another, mixing them up and creating interest. An example was for National Espresso Day, where special e-cards were sent with tag lines such as "Thanks a Latte" and "Sip Sip Hooray." As Lisa Dolan, SVP of Employee Engagement and Global Head of Diversity, Equity and Inclusion, says, "We want recognition and gratitude to be second nature as a way to say thank you and to celebrate successes. We've tried to encompass moments that matter to cover performance, values, humanity and just uplifting spirits."

- **Activity-related campaigns** – At Kelloggs, they had a campaign that linked to a wellbeing 5k challenge, where employees not only got involved with the activity but supported and recognized one another for achieving milestones and results through their recognition platform. Going back to the previous point about integration, this was a great way to not only drive recognition but link it naturally back to wellbeing.

At Key Forensics, they have a calendar of events used to plan Staff Appreciation Days throughout the year. Anything from National Chocolate Day to Eat a Red Apple Day, they use this as an opportunity to have a bit of fun, and at the same time, recognize their workforce. "The work we do can be hard and harrowing, so we use this as a way to show our people that we appreciate the great work they are doing," says HR Director Janet Hulme. A recent example was a campaign they did on National Fish & Chips Day, where vans turned up at each site to deliver the pre-chosen food they had ordered. "It created such a buzz and actually led to productivity increasing by 28% on that day!" says Hulme. This could have been because of the chemicals released from recognition or those from the fish, but either way, it was a great result!

Another example is at Missguided, where they created a campaign for World Kindness Day. On this day, they had a specially branded e-card designed so employees could recognize acts of kindness. For each e-card given, employees were entered into a special prize draw, and to deliver even more kindness, Missguided also donated money to a local food bank.

- **Appreciation day or week** – At HomeServe, they introduced a special weekly campaign called "Thank You Thursday," as a way to encourage employees to recognize one another. It was a huge success, in fact, often they'd have over 15,000 e-cards being sent on that one day. Over time, the recognition culture at Homeserve improved so much that recognition was a daily occurrence, so the team decided to retire the campaign. This is a great example of how to adapt and maintain your programs as the company culture changes, too.

  Another example is at Reward Gateway, where the team does something special to celebrate Employee Appreciation Day. In 2021, they held a global virtual recognition event, which they called the "Thank You Festival," doing so at a time when many of their employees were still in lockdown because of COVID-19. They wanted to do something special, something incredible, to make each and every employee feel appreciated and to celebrate the contributions the teams had been making. The event was a huge success, with 87% of employees sending or receiving recognition e-cards on the day, with the same number of appreciation moments being shared in one day as what was normally sent in a month.

Keep it fresh

Although I'm not the best gardener, I do know the importance of refreshing my garden, moving my plants around to give them more room to grow, and adding new plants to supplement the others to improve the overall appearance of my garden. The same is true with recognition, for it needs to be refreshed continually or else it'll become stagnant, and employees will stop engaging. Refreshing your programs could mean anything from changing them to removing them or even introducing new ones from time to time. Whatever you decide to do, it's important to take this step to create the recognition culture your people and business need and to meet your recognition objectives.

Here are some things to keep in mind as you refresh your recognition programs:

- **Take employee feedback seriously** – Start by listening to what your employees are saying and doing when it comes to recognition. Are there certain programs that are working and others that are not? Have they lost interest in a program, or is one of your recognition rewards not as meaningful as it needs to be? Use your employee feedback to strategically help you meet their needs and achieve your overall objectives.

  For example, in Chapter 3 I shared the story of how at a previous company we had special watches designed to recognize years of service. The feedback from our employees was that it wasn't valued, and we quickly changed the program to something that would make them feel appreciated.

- **Reflect new business objectives, commitments and challenges** – As mentioned throughout this book, recognition can drive business results. For this reason, it's important to constantly keep an eye on what your company's business objectives and challenges are, and refresh your recognition program and plans to drive the behaviors and actions that will help achieve them. For example, if your business is having problems related to safety, customer service, or sales, could they be addressed and overcome by creating new recognition plans or tools to embed these actions and behaviors into your employees' daily routines. Remember that recognition is a business tool, and use it over and over again to help your people and your business be successful.

  An example is what Roche Pharmaceuticals did to reflect a new business strategy called "One Roche," which was about encouraging a move from working independently to crossing over and sharing between the three business areas, doing so with a "One Roche" mindset. To drive this new behavior, they created a special e-card for employees to send to one another to recognize when employees showed how they were embracing the new mindset, reinforcing their behaviors through recognition.

Another example is what LinkedIn did with their new "Bravo! Distinguish" recognition plan that was launched in July 2021 to sit alongside their existing recognition plans. The plan is meant to support and drive their commitment to DIBS (diversity, inclusion and belonging), acting as a way to recognize the important work their 500 global employee volunteers are doing on top of their day jobs to support this important initiative.

- **Reflect on what's going on in the world** – Another thing to keep an eye on is what's happening in the world around you, bringing this into why and how you recognize your people. An example is how companies have been reacting and refreshing their recognition programs throughout the last few years during the COVID-19 pandemic. I've shared some examples earlier in this chapter, but here are a few more to highlight what companies have done:

The first example is Dunelm, who created a set of e-cards during the pandemic that had a home theme since people were spending more time at home and to align with their business as a home furnishing retailer. These e-cards focused on appreciating one another, being part of a team, looking out for each other, and doing well despite the circumstances. They were a huge success, with four times more of these e-cards being sent than in the past, showing the importance of recognizing and connecting with one another, especially during challenging times.

Another example is Welcome Break, who to thank their employees for their contributions during lockdown created their own version of the U.K. Thursday night clap for the NHS (National Health Services) celebration. They created a short "Clap for the Team" video that included each member of the leadership team saying thank you as they clapped, with the overall message being "tonight we clap for you."

Measure the impact

And finally, there's no way to tell if something is working without measurement. For a garden, you do this by looking at the size and health of your plants, and for recognition, it is very similar, as you look at the size and health of recognition in respect to usage and the overall impact on your people and your company.

There are many tools and techniques to help you measure the effectiveness and impact of your recognition program, from soliciting employee feedback to running surveys to holding focus groups. Whatever you decide to do, the key is to do it strategically. You should always have a goal in mind so you can measure against this regularly, and make measurement a part of your normal processes. Here are a few things to keep in mind as you do this:

1. **Have an adequate sample** – The first thing to do before measuring and analyzing your data is to make sure that you have an adequate sample size, for if you don't, you won't be getting a full picture of data. You can look at sample sizes in terms of size, but also in reach, meaning that your sample size should be from a diverse group of employees (leaders, managers, front-line employees, for example).

2. **Look for trends** – Once you're comfortable with the data, it's time to roll up your sleeves and start making some sense of it. Look for what statisticians call "thematic analysis," which are common themes, patterns and/or relationships that emerge from your data. Use these themes to understand what is working, not working, and opportunities for improvement.

   One word of caution is to look out for something called "confounding factors," which is when it looks like there is a correlation but there actually isn't. For example, let's say that for one month you notice that one of your sites is not sending out any e-cards. This could be because they aren't engaged with the program or it could be something else, like possibly there is a huge customer order that is making everyone work overtime and thus they haven't had time to recognize one another. In these situations, I suggest you have a quick chat with the site manager to understand what's going on before doing anything, helping them to find a solution that fits the situation and can support recognition even during a challenging time.

3. **Do something** – Last, but certainly not least, is to do something with what you've found and create a call-to-action. Think of this as your plan of what you're going to do to change the results when you measure it again. It can be a temporary measure, e.g. coming up with a specific campaign, or a long-term measure, e.g. changing a program to better meet the needs of your workforce, but whatever you come up with, it's important to quickly and thoroughly take it to the next step by actioning it.

An example of a company who does this is LinkedIn, who constantly look through the data and analytical lens when reviewing their recognition program. One example was when they found by analyzing their data that they were missing what they called a recognition award "sweet spot," as awards jumped from $30 to $150, and actions showed that they needed something in between to reflect the most appropriate levels of contribution. By adding in an award at $75 it did just this, and they told me that it's now the most used award level!

"We look at data every which way we can to look for opportunities to improve our program or to see what else needs to be done. We make the connections and we connect the data dots to make sure that our recognition program does what it 'says on the tin' to drive our business and foster our culture – which we believe is a real differentiator for us," said Katherine Gilbert, Senior Director, Compensation & Benefits EMEA/LatAm at LinkedIn.

Calls to Action:

Evaluate how well your "gardeners" are doing their jobs. Answer the following questions and create a plan for each as required:

Do our leaders and managers act as the role models that we need them to be? If not, what can we do to change this?

Do we have wellbeing champions that drive recognition effectively with their teams? If not, what can we do to change this?

Does our general workforce play their part in driving recognition? If not, what can we do to change this?

Evaluate how well your informal recognition "tools" are working to support your formal recognition program and meet your recognition objectives.

Which informal recognition tools are working well?

Which informal recognition tools need to be improved and if so, what can we do?

Which new informal recognition tools should we consider introducing?

Evaluate how well you are "maintaining" your recognition programs.

Doing well now:

Opportunities to improve:

Chapter 5: The Plays

To bring appreciation and recognition to life, this last chapter is devoted entirely to case studies, or "plays," since this book is called a playbook. And like a playbook, it contains a variety of approaches and ways to get things done.

You'll notice that I've included plays from companies of different sizes, locations and industries, and ones having very different recognition pyramids. This serves as a reminder to you that there is no one way to design a recognition pyramid and run your recognition program, and also to give you a wide variety of practical and tangible ideas. If you're like me, you'll end up with much of this chapter highlighted, using it to help you develop or refresh your recognition pyramid now and in the future.

Here are a few things to keep in mind when reading the plays in this chapter:

- **Each company is different**
  I know you'll be inspired by what these companies do, but resist the temptation to copy and paste this into what you do at your company. If your strategy and objectives are similar, by all means take inspiration from them, but then make it your own.

- **Each recognition pyramid is different**
  Following on from the previous point, you'll notice that each recognition pyramid is different. Some use all three of the levels plus a years of service plan, some just one, and some two. Even within a level, you'll see that some have one plan, while others have multiple plans. Keep in mind that one is not better than the other, they are all created based on the individual company's goals and strategy.

- **They all do much more**
  To make this book manageable, as I know we all have busy
  lives, I didn't share everything that each company does when
  it comes to recognition. I say this because I don't want you to
  think when reading them that this is all they do, for most if not
  all of them do so much more. I've tried to spread the topics
  between companies, thus sharing different ways to achieve
  similar objectives.

To help you quickly and easily see which levels each company has
in their recognition program, each play contains an image of their
pyramid. In addition, the following icons are used so you can see the
level for each of their individual recognition plans:

 Everyday recognition

 Above and Beyond recognition

 Best of the best recognition

 Years of service recognition

So without further ado, here are the 36 plays. Huge thanks to everyone
that let me interview them and share their wonderful and inspirational
stories on how we *Appreciate It!* around the world!

Abcam

COMPANY

An idea conceived in a University of Cambridge laboratory in 1998, Abcam has grown to be a global business that supports life science researchers in their quest to understand the cause of disease and ultimately offer improvements to diagnoses and treatments. To achieve this, Abcam develops and manufactures its own products in specialist facilities across the globe and sources from over 200 partners – offering scientists the newest, most innovative and highest quality biological research tools available globally.

Abcam has over 1,600 employees in four continents.

OVERVIEW

Abcam believes it's important to think differently, leaving complacency at the door, and always aiming higher. This is true in how it moves fast and pushes the boundaries to provide the materials that enable scientific achievements, and also in how the Company recognizes its global workforce in different ways to feel connected, recognized and valued.

One way they do this is by having just one level to their formal recognition program. "Over the last few years we have tried different approaches but they just didn't work. Our view is to keep it local and keep it real with our teams," says Nick Skinner, SVP Human Resources.

The organization complements this with a variety of non-traditional informal recognition. From a career development fund that recognizes individual needs to learn and grow, to its global employee share purchase plan that recognizes colleagues for their contributions to the growth of the Company, or by spending time with their very visible and knowledgeable CEO, there are many opportunities for recognition.

Another difference is Abcam's focus on the sharing and storytelling of recognition, doing so through their recognition platform, chat tool, plasma screens across the office and its weekly newsletter. "Storytelling is a big part of our culture, so we showcase our recognition stories relentlessly to share what employees have done and how they've been recognized. This gets advocacy from others, makes it visible and encourages people to recognize," says Skinner.

RECOGNITION PROGRAM

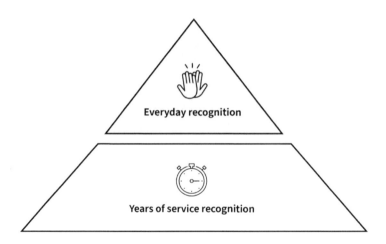

There are two levels and two individual plans in Abcam's "Recognise" recognition program:

 Anytime peer-to-peer e-cards: e-cards based on Abcam's three behaviors are available on their global recognition platform and can be sent by anyone at any time, to individuals or teams. They can be shared on the virtual, social recognition wall as well as through the chat tool, giving employees the opportunity to engage with the recognition moments.

"Our teams work globally, so it was important not to have a recognition solution that was site-based but global. This ensures we can value cross-functional, multi-disciplinary teams equally. The tool is great for this," says Skinner.

 Years of service recognition: Employees are recognized for their years of service each and every year. In the U.K. they receive an e-card along with an Amazon voucher for £15, which is the same regardless of years of service, while in the U.S. it is cupcakes and doughnuts. "We do this because it is no longer about lifetime service; but instead a chance each year to recognize the contribution and what they have learned," says Skinner.

TIPS

- **Don't be afraid to try something crazy.** As Henry Ford once said, "If you always do what you've always done, you'll always get what you've always got." An example is when Skinner went to the Abcam board with his proposal for their global share purchase plan. On the agenda it was titled "Crazy Idea," but it ended up being approved and now 93% of employees are enrolled in it. Abcam embraces and encourages bold innovation like this; one of the behaviors it uses to define its culture is "Audacious."

- **Don't worry about getting things perfect from the start.** At Abcam, one of their behaviors is "Agile," which is about "working with pace, purpose and a focus on quality and delivery, moving forward at the speed of life." You'll never be able to do this if you're always worrying about perfection.

Ascentis

COMPANY

Ascentis is one of the U.K.'s leading educational charities that transforms the lives of around 170,000 people every year through their range of qualifications and specialist software. They work closely with colleges, schools, independent training organizations and universities to design cutting-edge qualifications to enable people to progress to higher education and employment. Since 1975, they've been committed to enabling learning through innovative education and exceptional customer service, creating life-changing opportunities for all.

Ascentis has around 150 employees working in their head office in Lancaster as well as those working remotely throughout the U.K.

OVERVIEW

At Ascentis they're not only committed to creating life-changing experiences and opportunities for their customers, but also for their people. This is visible in their new head office in Lancaster, where they've designed experiential and fun-themed rooms such as the Alice in Wonderland and Harry Potter rooms, and also when it comes to their new "One Team" recognition program.

At each stage, employees don't just receive recognition, but experience it. Whether it's receiving celebration tickets, having a spin of the winning wheel, or having your photo taken up against the Halo recognition wall, there's no doubt that recognition moments are truly an experience that make employees feel valued and appreciated, and will be remembered.

RECOGNITION PROGRAM

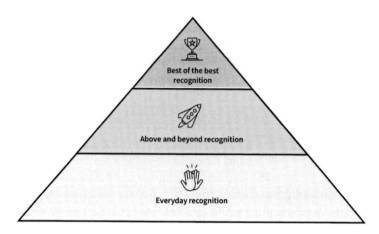

There are three levels and five individual plans in Ascentis's "One Team" recognition program:

 Anytime peer-to-peer social recognition: Everyday recognition is handled informally, with employees sending one another messages of praise through their online messaging tool.

 Anytime manager red celebration tickets: At the next level, managers can recognize employees at any time by giving them a special red celebration ticket for going above and beyond. Once they've collected three of these tickets, the employee gets to spin the winning wheel, where they can win prizes such as a day of annual leave, a treat basket, a double lunch break, cakes served in one of their themed rooms or even a secret lucky bag. Managers are encouraged to not only present these tickets to members of their team, but to those in other teams to encourage and support the One Team ethos.

Anytime leadership golden celebration tickets: Members of the leadership team can award an employee a special golden celebration ticket at any time, which is the equivalent of three red celebration tickets. This gives them an instant spin of the winning wheel rather than having to wait to collect additional red tickets.

 "Halo Award" - monthly leadership golden celebration ticket: At the end of the month, the heads of the departments and the leadership team review all of the social recognition and red celebration tickets which have been awarded, and select one employee to receive the Halo Award. The winner will receive a golden celebration ticket to spin the winning wheel, and also can have their picture taken if they desire at the Halo recognition wall. The award is also announced on screens throughout the office and on their online messaging tool, so employees can celebrate together and create opportunities for digital interaction.

 "Office Oscars" - annual peer-to-peer nomination awards: The top level of recognition is Ascentis's annual Office Oscars, which are linked to their company values. Anyone can nominate anyone for them, with the leadership team selecting winners for each of their values as well as for the manager and leader of the year.

Winners receive an Oscar trophy and £100 to donate to a charity of their choice, aligning it to their corporate social responsibility objectives, and giving employees the opportunity to do something that is meaningful to them.

These are announced and awarded at a big celebration event, with all those who have been nominated having their names appear on the boards to further celebrate their achievements.

TIPS

- **Take care in preparing for your leadership pitch.** When you go to your leadership team to gain their support, make sure that you not only show your enthusiasm and passion for what you are proposing, but also show the impact and difference that it will make.

- **Add some fun into the design of your recognition program.** Adding extra elements to a recognition program is great, but make sure that it is "fun with a reason," creating the experience and results that are important to your people and your business.

Atlantis Resorts Dubai

COMPANY

Nestled between the calm turquoise waters of the Arabian Gulf and the majestic Dubai skyline, Atlantis, The Palm is the crown of the world-famous Palm island in Dubai. It includes 1,548 guest rooms, 34 restaurants, and the world's largest waterpark.

Atlantis Resorts has approximately 2,800 permanent employees and 400 contractors who provide service to millions of guests per year.

OVERVIEW

Since opening its doors in 2008, Atlantis Resorts has created and delivered award-winning programs to reward and recognize excellence and to celebrate the people delivering it. They've done this in their own unique way through spectacular recognition events, to once-in-a-lifetime rewards such as stays at their hotel and meals at their restaurants that make their people feel genuinely appreciated, and at the same time, help them better understand their business and serve their customers.

"The beauty of working at Atlantis is that it's a village, and because of this anything we dream, we can do. We have a ballroom, 34 restaurants, an AV company, tailors, florists, etc. to help us run in-house recognition events at a fraction of the cost that are creative and original," says Kristina Vaneva, Director of Employee Engagement and Internal Communications.

But it isn't all about the excitement of the parties and rewards that have led to a 7% increase in employee engagement scores relating to recognition. It's also been by operating their programs through a diversity lens to ensure that all employees are treated in a fair and consistent way. Here are two ways they're doing this:

- **Segment awards –** At Atlantis they have several large and diverse divisions, ranging from rooms, to food, to Finance. To ensure there is fair representation across the divisions for recognition awards, they've created a schedule so that nominations come from different divisions each month. In addition, for each award they've created four categories that are broken out by job level (colleague, team leader, manager and director). "We do it this way because going above and beyond looks different at the different job levels, and we wanted to be fair to everyone," says Vaneva.

- **"Beautify" nominations –** With 87 different nationalities, for many of their employees English is not their first language. So for every nomination that is received for recognition awards, the HR team "beautifies" them, making sure that they all read well and thus all have equal chances for being selected as a winner.

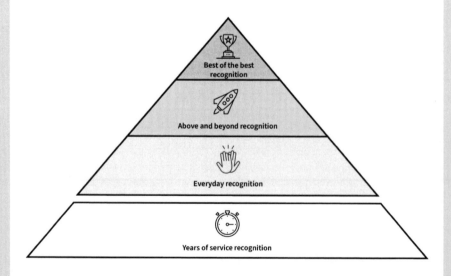

RECOGNITION PROGRAM

Best of the best recognition

Above and beyond recognition

Everyday recognition

Years of service recognition

There are four levels and four individual plans in Atlantis Resort's recognition program:

 Anytime peer-to-peer e-cards: In 2020, Atlantis changed their service philosophy, creating five new behaviors. To drive and support this, they introduced cards that can be given by anyone at any time for demonstrating one of the behaviors.

There are two parts of the card – the actual card with the recognition message which is given to the employee, and a tear-off part that is put into a raffle. Each month there are three winners who receive prizes such as resort experiences or popular tech gifts such as iPhones.

 "Atlantis Legend Awards" – monthly and quarterly nominated awards: The Atlantis Legend awards have been in place since 2009, and recognize and reward employees for top achievements through living their company values. Employees are nominated for these by managers, with the senior leadership team selecting the winners and runners up.

They celebrate these awards with spectacular theme-based lunch or dinner celebrations that include in-house decorations and entertainments. Amazing monetary and non-monetary rewards are given out, including a stay at their resort.

 "Atlantis Legend Awards" – annual peer-to-peer nominated awards: The top level of recognition are the annual Atlantis Legend Awards, which are selected from the best of the best quarterly winners. They again hold a spectacular event to celebrate these achievements, with winners and runners up again receiving high-value awards. For this top level recognition, the award is a trip for two to one of their parent-owned resorts along with money.

 Years of service recognition: Each year, Atlantis holds a loyalty party for employees with five and ten years of service. The event always has a unique theme, creating amazing experiences and everlasting memories. Attendees receive beautiful certificates along with awards - for five years they receive a voucher to spend at one of their restaurants, and for ten years they receive a night's stay with excursions at their resort. "Many of our colleagues would not be able to dedicate a portion of their salaries to eat or stay at our resort, so it is great for them to have this experience," says Vaneva.

TIPS

- **It's important to put the spotlight on recognition in your own way to celebrate the winners and showcase their achievements.** At Atlantis, they do this by calling award winners onto the stage to receive their certificate and to hear their recognition story. They also have a recognition wall which has photos of winners along with quotes taken from their nomination.

- **Focus on all aspects of your recognition events.** At Atlantis, they go the extra mile to make sure that every employee attending their recognition events has a good time and leaves feeling appreciated. This is achieved by ensuring managers attending understand the important role they have to play, and also by structuring the event to include activities to get everyone involved. As Vaneva explained, "It's the little things that can make all the difference."

Atlassian

COMPANY

Atlassian is an enterprise software company that develops products for software developers, project managers and content management. From medicine and space travel, to disaster response and pizza deliveries, their products help teams all over the planet advance humanity through the power of software.

Atlassian has over 6,000 employees globally working in infinite locations supporting over 21,000 customers.

OVERVIEW

Atlassian's recognition program has evolved over the years, but it's always been firmly based on the same core principles – a focus on recognition and not reward, driving behavioral change and an emphasis on storytelling. Over the years the Company has evolved it in the following ways:

- **Align with their values**: About four years ago the Company changed the program to tie it to their values, using it as a way to bring their values to life. "We wanted to make recognition meaningful and consistent, not a nice to have, but an essential part of our people operating system," says Dominic Price, Work Futurist at Atlassian.

- **Team awards**: One of Atlassian's values is "Play, as a team," which highlights the importance of teams to their business and people. For this reason, the organization added the ability to give "Kudos" awards to teams, celebrating and recognizing their combined contributions.

- **Gift categories**: Over the years, Atlassian has created categories of recognition awards that employees can self-select, adding their preferences into their staff directory so that everyone can see what they like and don't like. This helps the recognition sender select something that the receiver will truly value, still giving them the ability to add their personal touch.

- **Paying it forward**: A new gift category, called "Better Kudos," was added based on a suggestion made by employees that relates to charity donations. As Price explained, "not all employees or actions require a gift, some are better with a pay-it-forward charity donation." And to make it even better, Atlassian matches the value of the award that is given to the selected charity.

These changes, and the work they've done to create a recognition culture have paid off, with an average of three Kudos being sent each year by employees, and the overall number of Kudos sent over the last two years increasing significantly.

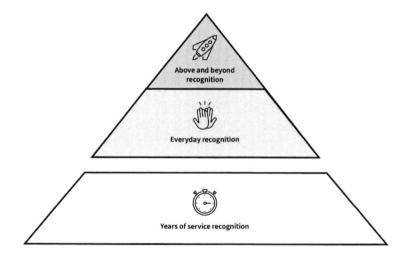

RECOGNITION PROGRAM

Above and beyond recognition

Everyday recognition

Years of service recognition

There are three levels and four individual plans in Atlassian's "Kudos" recognition program:

 Anytime peer-to-peer social recognition: For everyday recognition, the Company handles it informally, making it instantaneous and easy to give and get involved with through the online messaging tool. They created special recognition and values emojis to add to the fun and drive interaction.

 Anytime peer-to-peer "Kudos Awards" - anytime peer-to-peer awards: All employees can send Kudos awards at any time to anyone across the organization for going above and beyond based on living their company values. No approval is required to send one, and there is no maximum number of awards that can be sent.

The award amounts are loosely based on the tax laws for each country, e.g. below the amount which involves taxing the employee for receiving the gift, making it an easier and more seamless experience for the employee. As mentioned in the overview, the sender can select which reward to give based on what the individual has set up under their reward profile.

 "Big Kudos Awards" - anytime peer-to-peer awards: All employees can send Big Kudos Awards at any time to anyone across the organization for doing what Price calls "a wow, this is huge thing" or something that requires the story being told. The amount is higher for this award, between around $100-300 AUD, and is selected based on the magnitude of the behavior and action.

Since at Atlassian it's the story that is important, Big Kudo stories are shared during the monthly global town hall call, with the sender telling the story and sharing the positive behaviors.

Years of service recognition: Employees are recognized for three, five and 10 years of service. For three and five years, their names and photos are shared during the "congratlassian" part of the Friday global town hall meeting, with stories being shared at local town halls or meetings. They also receive a bit of extra leave during their anniversary year, which they are then asked to share in a blog about what they have done during this time off.

For 10 years of service, their story is shared during the Friday meeting, and they also receive a personalized bobblehead, with one copy going to the employee and the other put onto the bobblehead shelf, becoming a part of the company folklore.

TIPS

- **Recognition will not stick if your leaders do not lead the way, going first to demonstrate and role model it.** For this reason, it's important to get into the hearts and minds of your leaders when it comes to recognition, understanding and feeling the behavioral changes required to create a recognition culture.

- **It's critical for recognition to be authentic and meaningful to the people you are delivering it to.** Get out there and talk to your employees to understand what they want and what they need, and then design your authentic recognition program to match this. As Price says, "open your ears and listen to your employees."

Burton's Biscuit Company

COMPANY

Burton's Biscuit Company (Burton's) is a British biscuit (cookies) manufacturer. They are recognized in the U.K. as the second-biggest supplier of biscuits, and home to the U.K.'s most iconic brands such as "Wagon Wheels™, Jammie Dodgers™, Maryland Cookies™, Thomas Fudge's™, Paterson's™, Lyons™, Fish' n' Chips™ and Royal Edinburgh™.

Burton's has over 2,000 employees located across six sites in the U.K.

OVERVIEW

When Burton's decided to review and update their recognition program, they set out to create something consistent and inclusive. Consistent, as different approaches and processes were followed across the various bakeries, and inclusive, as much of their recognition program focused on their head office employees, representing only 30% of their total workforce. So to adhere to the inclusive approach, they developed the program by taking on feedback from their leadership team as well as their overall workforce through focus groups and surveys.

The result is their "Bake My Day" digital recognition and communication platform, with individual plans similarly having cookie-related names such as the "Treat Award," "Crumbs Up Award" (a pun on Thumbs Up) and "Smart Cookie Award." According to Helen Cummings, Group Communications & Engagement Manager, "We enjoy a good pun at Burton's and love to have some fun, so we had to make sure our new platform reflected this!"

They've also been inclusive in how they made sure bakery employees don't miss out on recognition since the majority don't have access to a company phone or laptop. One way was by sending postcards and letters to employees' home addresses so they didn't miss the program's launch. Another was by having a live feed of the recognition awards from the social recognition wall to the T.V.s located across the bakeries so they can be a part of recognition even while baking cookies.

And finally, each week, their HR Director sends an email, and posters go up across the bakeries with the names of those given Treat Awards, encouraging others to nominate the following week. "This means we can celebrate achievements together as One Team, helping all of our employees feel valued and receive the recognition they deserve. As a result, we can retain our amazing employees and reinforce behaviors aligned with our values," says Cummings.

The new recognition program has been successful in achieving their objectives, creating a simple, consistent way of recognizing their workforce wherever they work. And since the launch of Bake My Day, they've had a 168% increase in recognition being made, received great feedback from managers and employees, Glassdoor scores have gone from 3.9 to 4.7, and they've already seen a decrease in turnover.

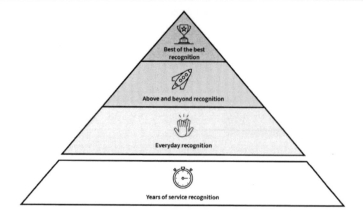

RECOGNITION PROGRAM

Best of the best recognition

Above and beyond recognition

Everyday recognition

Years of service recognition

There are four levels and five individual plans in Burton's "Bake My Day" recognition program:

 "Treat Awards" - anytime peer-to-peer e-cards: Burton's has two types of e-cards, or what they call Treat Awards, that employees can send to one another at any time through their recognition platform. The first are e-cards that align with their values, and the second are greetings that help to connect their workforce.

 "Crumbs Up Awards" - anytime peer-to-peer financial awards: The next level are the Crumbs Up Awards, which is where employees can nominate one another at any time through their recognition platform. Once approved, the employee receives £10 to spend on their recognition platform.

 "Treat Awards" - quarterly peer-to-peer nominated awards: Each quarter, site leaders look through all of the Treat Awards given, and select the top winners, awarding them £100 to spend on their recognition platform. There is no formal limit of how many can be awarded, it is up to the discretion of each site to select those that are worthy of receiving this award.

"Smart Cookie Awards" - anytime director awards:
The top level are the Smart Cookie Awards, which can be
given by one of their 12 directors at any time to recognize
their team for going above and beyond. They have the
discretion to award between £10 to £200, which again can
be spent through their recognition platform.

 Years of service recognition: Currently Burton's approach
to recognizing years of service is not consistent across the
sites. This will be reviewed and addressed during the next
phase of their recognition review, applying a similar
consistent and inclusive approach.

TIPS

- **Consider having a working group help you launch
  your program.** They can not only help you not only
  understand what will work at their site, but create the
  energy and buzz to get people involved.

- **Take advantage of FOMO (fear of missing out)**. Share
  and broadcast recognition so that people will want to get
  involved and be a part of it for as the acronym says, they
  won't want to miss out.

C Space

COMPANY

C Space is a Customer Agency on a mission to change the world of business by proving that stronger relationships build stronger businesses. They do this by bringing the "outside in," working with the customers of their 200+ clients around the world to surface insights which drive impact and growth.

C Space has approximately 400 employees located in the U.S. and the U.K.

OVERVIEW

When C Space co-created their new set of values, shortly after a merger and rebranding of the organization, they decided that one way to bring them to life was through a new recognition program. Not just any recognition program, but one that would be used as a strategic business tool. "We see recognition as a strategic tool for shaping our culture and behaviors, positively reinforcing and celebrating what we achieve and what we want to see more of," says Phil Burgess, Global Chief People Officer.

One way they ensured their program achieved these objectives was by moving to a digital recognition platform, making recognition something that can easily be done across groups and geographies as the business grows, removing barriers and supporting their strategy of "better together." The platform also helps them leverage the power of social recognition, with recognition moments being shared across the business to drive collaboration, build relationships, drive business awareness and overall results. "We used to recognize using physical cards (and we still do this!), but we realized we were limiting the flow of positive recognition across the company between people working in different locations. We weren't getting the 'halo effect' where social recognition can showcase and influence others. That became even more important for us during the COVID-19 pandemic when we effectively became a remote organization overnight," says Burgess.

They've also been meeting their recognition objectives by continually evolving their programs to drive the desired results. An example is with their "Impact Awards," a biannual celebration to recognize the impact C Space employees were having on their clients. Initially, Impact Awards were only awarded for commercially-focused achievements, something the C Space leadership team wanted teams to focus on because it was correlated with client satisfaction and retention. Over time, they heard from employees that they felt this approach ultimately excluded some people and teams who were making an impact in other ways. They brought a working group together to review and refresh this plan, and came up with a new one that recognizes based on four different categories: Commercial Impact, Social Impact, Cultural Impact and IN.pact, which is for teams working on projects that had a big impact within C Space, such as HR, Operations and Engineering. "Some teams were feeling like unsung heroes, so by changing the plan and reframing how we thought about impact, we were able to develop a more inclusive approach, giving all those contributing to making an impact the opportunity to be recognized," says Burgess.

Alongside their regular program and rituals, and in the spirit of constant evolution and keeping things fresh, C Space also introduced signature recognition moments during the year. For example, when everyone across the business was really pulling out the stops for clients, they wanted to recognize them for their efforts and encourage them to take some time to themselves. They rewarded everyone with a "Me Day," a day off with a small budget to spend on something meaningful to them. Wherever possible they tie these signature moments to their company values. One of these is "We Before Me" and the Me Day was a reframe of this, reminding people that sometimes it's important to focus on self care in order to be able to show up well for your team.

RECOGNITION PROGRAM

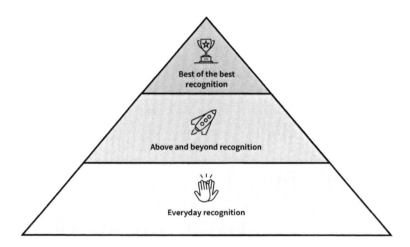

There are three levels and three individual plans in C Space's recognition program:

 Anytime peer-to-peer e-cards: C Space has two types of e-cards that employees can send to one another at any time through their recognition platform. The first are e-cards that align with their values, and the second are celebratory ones which help boost morale even from afar including, "Happy Anniversary," "Welcome" and "Congratulations."

 Anytime team leader discretionary awards: The next level is awards that team leaders can give at any time to recognize their people for going above and beyond. They have discretion when it comes to timing, and also in respect to what they give. From gift cards, to a night out, to a spot bonus, to a day off, to training, team leaders are allocated a small budget to decide what is best to help individuals feel appreciated and valued.

 "Impact Awards" - annual peer-to-peer nominated awards: The final level is the annual Impact Awards, which are awarded based on four categories. Employees nominate themselves or others for these awards, with a jury selecting three finalists for each category, and then the winners being voted on by the entire organization. The three winners for each category receive $2,000, then $1,000 and finally $500. They celebrate the winners and their stories in a video which is shared on social media as well as part of the onboarding process to showcase their recognition culture to new employees.

TIPS

- **It's important to evolve your recognition program.** Ensure you're keeping it fresh and authentic to your business and your people. An example is C Space's Impact Awards, which changed recently. But as Burgess explained, it's still not perfect, so after each round they pause and evaluate it, making changes to continually improve on it.

- **Don't be afraid to change things in the middle if it's not working.** An example is again with C Space's Impact Awards. When they first opened it up for nominations it was only the individual who could nominate themselves. When they found that many people didn't feel comfortable doing this, they quickly changed the process, letting anyone nominate people for these awards.

Certis Security

Certis Security (Certis) is one of Asia's largest security companies responsible for designing, building and operating multi-disciplinary smart security and integrated services. Their multi-service offering leverages their strong heritage in security, and is augmented by applied AI solutions that form part of their comprehensive technology development and systems integration capabilities that are fully cyber secure by design.

Certis has over 27,000 employees located in six countries across the world.

When SNP Security in Australia was acquired by global company Certis in 2018, they wanted to use recognition as a way to help their 3,400 employees through what can be a challenging time of uncertainty. "We knew that people were nervous about what was going to happen with the acquisition, so we wanted something to say 'hey guys here's something for you', something to show them that we cared about them, and at the same time, get them excited about now working for Certis" says Rosanna Paratschek, National Manager – Remuneration & Benefits.

The new program, called "Certis RnB" (standing for recognition and benefits) was introduced in two phases, with the first phase focusing on creating a culture of recognition, one where people thanked one another, and the second phase moving into the reward part of recognition. It was launched through a country-wide roadshow, going out to the front line to spread the word on the new program. "We sat in break rooms with bowls of lollies, enticing people to come over and learn more about the program and how they could get involved," says Paratschek.

Another way Certis "sells" recognition to their dispersed workforce is through various e-card campaigns, sending all employees recognition e-cards to mark specific events throughout the year. A recent example was on "R U OK Day," a day that encourages employees to question themselves and others, and which this past year (September 2021) was an unusually difficult time with Australians battling bushfires, floods and a global pandemic. For this reason, special "R U OK" e-cards were sent to their entire workforce to connect and encourage them during this challenging time, along with a company-wide campaign and pledge to find ways to check in and connect with each other.

RECOGNITION PROGRAM

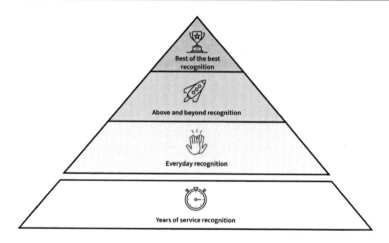

There are four levels and five individual plans in Certis's recognition program:

 "Say Cheers to Your Peers" - anytime peer-to-peer e-cards: The level of recognition are Certis's Say Cheers to Your Peers e-cards. They represent their seven values in addition to other greetings (e.g. Happy Birthday, Thank You, Congratulations, Welcome to the Team, Well Done). They can be sent by anyone at any time, and can be shared on their virtual social recognition wall.

"Values e-cards were a great way to introduce our new Certis values. Because they are front and center on Certis RnB now, most employees can easily rattle them off," says Paratschek.

"RnB Awards" - anytime manager awards: The next level are the RnB Awards, which managers can send out at any time to reward employees for doing a great job and demonstrating their company values. Employees receive $30 AUD to spend through their recognition platform, with no approval being required. The amount was intentionally set low, as they wanted to encourage frequent recognition.

Anytime senior managing director awards: The next level is discretionary awards, which any of the Senior Leadership Team members can give at any time to employees. The amount is discretionary, being determined by the leader approving it, and employees again receive credits to use through their recognition platform.

"Pinnacle Awards" - annual peer-to-peer nominated awards: The final level is the prestigious Certis Pinnacle Awards, a global award for employees at Certis around the world. Once a year, employees can nominate one another based on selected categories which tie back to their values, with one individual and one team selected as winners for each category. Winners receive a trophy, a letter from the

Group CEO, a cash prize and are invited to attend a ceremony in their Singapore headquarters. In addition, anyone nominated receives an e-card, and finalists receive $100 AUD loaded onto their recognition platform. After the ceremony, each week they share the stories of all finalists, celebrating their individual achievements and accomplishments.

 Years of service recognition: Each anniversary is acknowledged with a Happy Anniversary e-card. Anniversaries of five, 10, 15 years, etc. are managed outside the program and celebrated at the department level. Recipients of these awards receive an anniversary pin and a letter of congratulations from the Chief Executive. Service anniversaries for 20, 25, 30 years, etc., are celebrated at a special morning tea and are presented to the recipients by the Chief Executive.

TIPS

- **It's important to begin your recognition journey by creating a culture of recognition, a culture of appreciation.** By easing employees into recognition this way, the reward aspect of recognition will come more naturally and easily, ultimately being more effective. This is what Certis did in their two-phase approach, which has worked well for in the last 12 months, 84.5% of their employees have either sent or received recognition or both.

- **When rolling out your recognition program, it's important to put effort into educating your managers, getting their buy-in and support, and getting them on board by winning their hearts and minds.** At Certis, they focused their attention on their frontline employees during their initial launch, and said that in hindsight they would have put the same, if not more, focus on their managers. Since then, they've incorporated this into manager training and communications to overcome this hurdle.

Charles Tyrwhitt

COMPANY

Charles Tyrwhitt, which rhymes with "spirit," is a multi-channel British retailer specializing in men's clothing. The Company was founded in 1986 by Nicholas Charles Tyrwhitt Wheeler and has a mission to "make it easy for men to dress well" and believe in doing things "properly" when it comes to their product, people and the planet.

Charles Tyrwhitt has just over 700 employees located in three countries, however they sell their products worldwide.

OVERVIEW

At Charles Tyrwhitt, one of the behaviors that sits alongside their company values is "I celebrate and champion my colleagues – together we win!" And over the years the team has developed a recognition program that they call "3 Cheers for The Tyrwhitteers" that does just this, celebrating and recognizing both small and big wins for individuals, teams and the company.

The program has changed over the years, becoming more meaningful and relevant to their people and the business. Here are two examples of how the Company has done this:

- The first is by moving to a digital recognition platform to create a more seamless and engaging recognition experience. The platform is called "The Celebration Station," and it hosts the individual recognition plans.

- The second is by evolving its recognition plans to adapt and focus on business objectives and priorities. An example is in how the "Tick from Nick" plan changed from being a quarterly award recognizing supporting charities, to one that can be given at any time and recognizes both charitable and wider CSR (Corporate Social Responsibility) work, aligning with their CSR "Be the Change" initiative. Winners have included employees who have reduced plastic usage, designed shirts using recyclable polyester and reduced CO_2 freight emissions, to name a few.

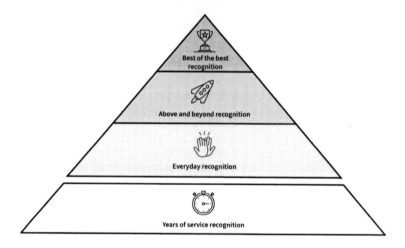

There are four levels and five individual plans in Charles Tyrwhitt's recognition program:

 Anytime peer-to-peer e-cards: Charles Tyrwhitt has two kinds of e-cards. The first are their 12 "Living our Values" e-cards, which include one for each of the three values, or what they call "BE-liefs," and then three each for the "BE-haviors" that go along with each BE-lief. This unique approach ensures that employees understand and recognize not just the value, but the behaviors that sit within it.

In addition, they have e-cards that recognize and celebrate occasions and activities. These include birthdays, anniversaries and achievements such as hitting key financial targets.

"Shout Outs from Leadership" - anytime leadership e-cards: To go along with the peer-to-peer e-cards, the Company created Shout Outs from Leadership e-cards, which consist of individually designed e-cards for each member of the leadership group. "They are designed to reflect something funny, interesting or engaging about each leader, injecting their personality and making them appear more human. They also break down barriers and connect them to our people," says Sam Shaw, Employee Communications and Engagement Manager.

For example, the Shout Out from Phil Vickers, Director of HR, is an image of a cup of tea. "When someone had done something really well I'd often do the small thing of making them a cup of tea and saying 'Thanks' at the same time. The e-card picked up on that and reflected something personal I was already doing. We wanted the leadership cards to feel genuine and different to the others." says Vickers.

 "Tick from Nick Awards" - anytime peer-to-peer nominated awards: The next is the "Tick from Nick" awards. Anyone can nominate anyone to receive one of these at any time, and they are given to employees doing work relating to the CSR agenda as well as charitable work.

Founder Nick Wheeler reads out all nominations and winners at business meetings to showcase these achievements and contributions, and delivers the award trophy in person. In addition, winners receive a special gift related to their work such as a free ticket to The Prince's Trust award finals for charity-related work.

 "Make it Easy Awards" - annual peer-to-peer nominated awards: Aligning with their mission "to make it easy for men to dress well," Charles Tyrwhitt has their Make it Easy awards. These recognize the best examples of Making it Easy at a special meal with the founder and CEO, with one person being selected as the overall champion and receiving a special prize.

Years of service recognition: At Charles Tyrwhitt they celebrate and recognize for every five years of service. Employees receive three things as part of the award, the first is money to spend on the discounts platform, and the second is an e-card from the Founder that has been personalized by including things specific to the employee. And finally, at business meetings, employees are presented with a metal sculpture that is shaped like a button and has a hole in the middle to hold pens. Employees receive bronze for five years, silver for 10, gold for 15 and platinum for 20 years, all of which can be stacked upon each other. To showcase and celebrate long service, in the reception area there are black and white photos of all employees hitting these milestone years.

TIPS

- **It's important to personalize recognition as much as possible.** Charles Tyrwhitt has done this by personalizing messages such as e-cards from their leaders, as well as awards given for the Tick from Nick program. This connects with employees in a different and more meaningful way.

- **It's important to keep it simple by not overcomplicating your recognition programs.** "The more you do this, the more your people will get involved and get engaged with recognition," says Vickers.

Chelsea Football Club

COMPANY

Chelsea Football Club (Chelsea FC), nicknamed "the Blues," is among England's most successful clubs competing in the Premier League, the top division of English football. Since being founded in 1905, they have won over 30 competitive honors, including six league titles and eight European trophies between their men's and women's teams.

Chelsea FC has 750 permanent and 1,200 sessional employees.

OVERVIEW

After Chelsea FC developed their six values, their "one-team ethos," they moved next to creating a recognition program to be an extension of these values, backing them up by capturing and recognizing employees for their achievements against them.

"By recognizing colleagues against our values, everyone has the equal opportunity to be recognized for helping us reach our goals and succeeding together," says Sara Matthews, Director of Human Resources.

RECOGNITION PROGRAM

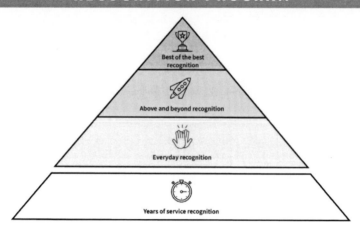

There are four levels and four individual plans in Chelsea FC's recognition program:

Anytime peer-to-peer e-cards: The first part of the recognition program that was put in place were values-based e-cards, which are available on their recognition platform, and can be sent by anyone at any time. "We put these in place as a way to say thank you for just doing good stuff, which we could do more of," says Matthews.

"Pride of Chelsea" - quarterly peer-to-peer nominated awards: The next level of recognition are the quarterly Pride of Chelsea' awards. Anchored by their value "Proud to be Chelsea," which talks about being part of something internationally recognized and admired, these awards recognize employees for going above and beyond in living any of their six values. Anyone can nominate a colleague to receive an award, with a panel of employees selecting runners-up and winners. There is no set number of winners, being flexible based on the achievements which have been put forward. "We didn't want to force fit it, as this just doesn't work. We wanted to retain as much flexibility where one quarter we might have a number of really great submissions we want to recognize versus another quarter where there is one stand out winner," says Matthews.

All winners receive certificates, a bottle of champagne or alternative, and additional gifts based on the level of the award. For team awards and gifts, they ask employees what they want, e.g. a team event, something for their area, etc., selecting something that is based on their preferences.

 "Pride of Chelsea" - annual awards: The top level of recognition are the annual Pride of Chelsea awards. For these, they celebrate all of the quarterly winners along with other nominations that they feel have stood out, doing so during a presentation ceremony. The executive team selects the winners independently based on a summary of the nomination. This is followed by a roundtable discussion until everyone agrees on the winner and runners up, who again receive certificates, champagne and cash to spend on gifts of their choice.

 Years of service recognition: Service recognition starts at 10 years' service, and then at 15, 20, 30, 40 and even 50 years. Colleagues receive a cash award linked to their service milestone in addition to attending a recognition event hosted by the Club Chairman. The most recent was an afternoon tea in the Director's Lounge in the stadium.

TIPS

- **Link your recognition programs to something tangible, like your company values**. By doing this, you can use your recognition program as a tool to further embed what's important to your business and your culture.

- **Consider being flexible on the number of award winners selected.** When determining your recognition award winners, consider being flexible on the final number being selected so that you focus on achievements and not a magic number.

Deloitte

Deloitte is a leading global provider of professional services, having dedicated professionals in independent firms throughout the world collaborating to provide audit and assurance, consulting, risk and financial advisory, risk management, tax, and related services to clients. They are led by a purpose to make an impact that matters – to their clients, to society and to their people.

Deloitte Australia has approximately 12,000 employees across the country.

OVERVIEW

Deloitte Australia has had a recognition program in place for about eight years. However, as Breckon Jones, Head of Employee Experience, explained, "Initially, it was very basic and was top-down, with only partners being able to recognize more junior people. It was, however, still more than what most companies in Australia had in place at the time."

Taking learnings from previous organizations which included American Express and Unilever, Jones revamped the program when he joined in 2019, doing so by adding additional levels to the existing "ShoutOut!" recognition program, focusing on peer-to-peer recognition at every level. It is now a highly effective and widely used program, with approximately 80,000 recognition moments being sent each year by their 12,000 employees.

One reason they've achieved such fantastic results is because they integrate recognition into the performance experience, linking and embedding it into their performance management processes. For example, when a goal is met and is noted in the performance management platform, there is a link provided to take the manager or colleague directly to the recognition platform. Here, they can easily and quickly recognize one another for achieving this goal. "We don't want people to have to search for things, so we've tried to package it all together within the flow of work, making it easier to do the things we want our people to do. The result is a continuous and full circle performance management (and recognition) experience for our employees," says Jones.

RECOGNITION PROGRAM

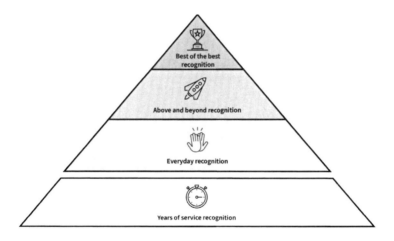

There are four levels and seven individual plans in Deloitte Australia's "ShoutOut!" recognition program:

 Anytime peer-to-peer e-cards: Deloitte has created a suite of e-cards that can be sent through their recognition platform. Front and center are those that reflect their company values, as well as the individual behaviors that underpin each value.

Sitting underneath these are two other sets of e-cards. The first are called "moments that matter," and are used to recognize supporting clients. The second are those that celebrate a variety of events such as joining the company, birthdays, career milestones, etc.

"High Fives," "Round of Applause" and "Standing Ovations" - anytime peer-to-peer nominated awards: Next are three levels of points-based awards that are given to recognize demonstrating their company values. Employees can nominate one another for these at any time, with a wizard within the platform helping them determine which is the most appropriate level based on the impact of the action. The budget holder approves the award, with the recipient receiving points to be used on their recognition platform.

"Innovation Awards" – annual peer-to-peer nominated awards: Deloitte's next recognition plan is the annual Innovation Awards, which are given to individuals who have demonstrated innovation. Employees can nominate one another for these awards, with a panel selecting the winners who receive points which again can be used through the recognition platform.

"CEO Awards" – annual peer-to-peer nominated awards: And finally, the newest plan at the top of the pyramid is the annual CEO Awards, which are given to employees who make an impact on the community. This supports the company's purpose to make an impact that matters, which for this award relates to an impact on society. Employees can nominate one another for these awards, with a panel selecting winners who receive points to be spent on the recognition platform.

Years of service recognition: At three years of service, and for every two year service milestone thereafter, employees receive a personalized yearbook to celebrate and recognize their time with the company. The yearbook includes stories and videos that have been contributed by team members, making it a one-of-a-kind and meaningful keepsake. In addition, employees receive points of increasing value for each service anniversary to be spent on the recognition platform.

TIPS

- **When it comes to recognition, it's important to start, no matter how big or small.** As Jones says, "Get that snowball rolling!" to ensure that your people feel appreciated and valued through your recognition programs and practices.

- **It's important to spend time on your recognition language and branding.** Develop something that will drive awareness and engagement with your program by being "impactful, emotive and sticky," says Jones. At Deloitte they've done this by naming their program ShoutOut!, something which has become a part of their natural language and ways of working.

EU Automation

COMPANY

EU Automation supplies the manufacturing world with parts, specializing in obsolete parts. They have over 20,000 customers located in 164 countries, and have a mission to supply the manufacturing world with industry-leading parts, service and speed so that manufacturers can continue doing what they do best – make manufacturing possible.

EU Automation has 250 employees located in the U.K., Germany, U.S. and Singapore.

OVERVIEW

EU Automation is all about supplying the world with parts and as of September 2021, they have a set of values that form the acronym PART, with the hashtag #PlayYourPART. However when it came to recognition, according to Alex Darby, Head of People, they didn't have the right internal parts. "When I joined the company, the only formal way we recognized our people was with an annual awards ceremony that recognized the same salespeople year after year. This was uninspiring and unmotivational for all those not winning and especially those in our very important operation and service teams. It also didn't align with our values. Additionally, like most, through the pandemic we also had to navigate a completely new way of working, which taught us a lot and highlighted the need for small token rewards as motivational tools, but also wellbeing gestures done in real time." says Darby.

Their new and evolving recognition program is now solidly aligned with their values, and is changing the culture to be one where recognition happens within and across teams. Although it's still early days and the program will continue to adapt (one of their values), the changes they've made so far with their new recognition parts are driving the change they'd hoped to see.

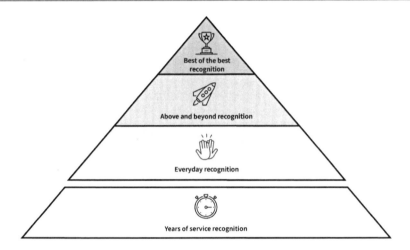

RECOGNITION PROGRAM

Best of the best recognition

Above and beyond recognition

Everyday recognition

Years of service recognition

There are four levels and five individual plans in EU Automation's recognition program:

 Anytime peer-to-peer e-cards: Employees can send e-cards to one another at any time. There are a set of e-cards that align with their four values, and another set that are changed every quarter to align with specific business or people focuses.

 "Shout Out Awards" - monthly leadership awards: The next level is their Shout Out non-financial awards, which are given by members of the Senior Leadership Team (SLT) to employees for going above and beyond in living the company values and contributing to the business. They are selected during a monthly meeting and shared publicly in their new company newsletter.

 "Pick Me Up Awards" - anytime manager awards: These awards started during COVID-19 as a way to lift the spirits of employees, thanking them for their contributions during a challenging time. They decided to keep them going, with managers being able to tap into their "pick me up pot" and reward their people when they demonstrate a value and want to send them a little something extra. HR approves the awards, but managers have complete discretion to select the personalized gift, with the value being no more than £50 or equivalent.

 "#PlayYourPART Awards" - annual awards: The final level is the annual Play Your Part Awards. At the end of the year, they have SLT nominated awards, Director nominated awards and peer voted awards. Nominees' stories are shared during the awards ceremony and then the winners are announced, thus celebrating everyone's contributions.

 Years of service recognition: Employees receive an e-card to celebrate their anniversary each year. In addition, they are currently reviewing and creating more ways to celebrate years of service every five years.

TIPS

- **Recognize against your company values as a way to embed them**. It's important to design your recognition program around your company values, using it as a way to embed them into how you recognize actions and behaviors.

- **Get your leadership team involved in recognition, giving them responsibility and accountability.** At EU Automation they've done this by having certain recognition plans owned by their senior leadership team, sending the message that they have an important part to play in driving a recognition culture.

Heineken

COMPANY

Founded in 1864 in Amsterdam, today, Heineken is one of the world's largest brewers, serving over 25 million beers each day across over 190 markets. They believe that quality is measured not in the size of their brand but in the purity of their beer, having an uncompromising passion for consumers and customers, enjoyment of life, the courage to dream and pioneer and care for people and the planet.

They have over 84,000 colleagues located across the globe, with 2,400 located in the U.K.

OVERVIEW

Back in 2018, with only 40 prizes of £1,000 available each year to a workforce of 2,400, Heineken U.K.'s recognition program was only reaching 2% of their colleagues. And because of this, according to their annual engagement survey, only 20% answered positively to the question "I receive recognition when I do a good job."

Armed with this data, and comments from colleagues saying they wanted recognition throughout the year, appreciation for going the extra mile, and to be able to share and celebrate success across the company, they set out to develop a modern, flexible and values-led recognition program with the following objectives:

• Move away from large awards for few to smaller awards for many.

• Make recognition happen on a more timely basis.

- Provide recognition that could apply to all colleagues.

- Maximize value from their budget.

- Create a single company-wide approach with pre-agreed budgets that allows local ownership and decision-making on the timing and level of awards.

- Provide more flexibility and the opportunity to recognize colleagues in different ways.

The result was a new online recognition program that they call "BREWards & Recognition" that recognizes different levels of achievement, bringing it all together in a seamless journey to meet the needs of their diverse and dispersed workforce. Since the launch in January 2019, 98% of colleagues have actively used BREWards & Recognition, with a total of 6,700 awards being issued, recognizing and celebrating the demonstration of the Heineken behaviors.

Besides the redesign of the recognition program, the key to their success has been the following:

- **Recognition champions** - Each business area has assigned one colleague as a recognition champion, making them responsible for owning and driving recognition in their part of the organization. This includes working with local management to review and approve awards, ensuring all colleagues are aware of the program, and proactively managing it so that recognition is fairly and consistently managed.

- **Videos** - The Reward team developed short how-to videos which they put on their in-house training platform. These ensure that colleagues can easily find and understand how to use the various elements of the program.

RECOGNITION PROGRAM

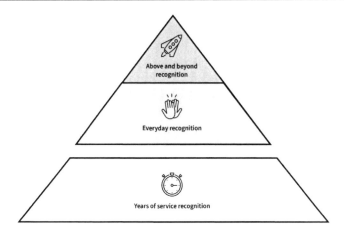

There are three levels and four individual plans in Heineken U.K.'s recognition program:

 Anytime peer-to-peer e-cards: These are available on their recognition platform, and can be sent by anyone at any time, and shared on their virtual social recognition wall. By doing this it aligns with a key element of the Heineken behaviors, "We play to win and celebrate success."

 "Cheers!" Awards - anytime manager awards: The next level is Cheers! Awards, which people managers can send out at any time at their discretion to reward individuals in their team or any other part of the business. The colleague instantly receives £50 to spend on the BREWards & Recognition platform, with no approval being required.

 "IPA" Awards - anytime peer-to-peer nominated awards: To further encourage peer-to-peer recognition, Heineken has Inspiring People Awards (IPA), being a play on Indian Pale Ale. For these awards, colleagues can nominate one another for going above and beyond. They can receive from £100 to £1,000 to be spent on the BREWards & Recognition platform or a day off work, or a dinner at one of their pubs. Recognition champions from each function review and approve nominations with their leadership team, along with the frequency and amounts. Some functions give them out as and when they come in, while others do it quarterly or annually.

"We got creative with our non-financial recognition to make our money go further and meet our objectives. A day off work or dinner at one of our pubs is entirely relevant for our people, and supports a business aim of encouraging colleagues to use our pubs and introduce friends and family to them," says Aileen Newall, Head of Reward.

 Years of service recognition: At Heineken U.K., they recognize 25 and 35 years of service, rewarding employees with a monetary value to spend on the BREWards & Recognition platform. In 2022, they are reviewing and revising this plan, determining how best to recognize years of service going forward.

TIPS

- **Look for opportunities to refresh and revamp how and where your program appears on your company's intranet.** At Heineken they moved their social recognition wall from the recognition page to the home page, creating more interest and engagement with the program.

- **Take advantage of local supporters by establishing formal or informal recognition champions.** At Heineken they've done this as a way to drive recognition locally, extending the reach and impact of the program.

HomeServe

COMPANY

HomeServe is one of the U.K.'s leading home assistance providers, living their mission of "freeing our customers from the worry and inconvenience of home emergency repairs" since 1993. From cover and new boilers to one-off repairs, their iconic red vans are on the roads caring for their over 1.6 million customers through a range of products and services.

HomeServe has 2,500 employees located in five offices plus remote workers across the U.K.

OVERVIEW

HomeServe has been on a journey since 2015 to shine a spotlight on achievements and create a recognition culture. They've done this by evolving and expanding their recognition program, named "STAR" (Special Thanks and Recognition), being led by a strategy of "keeping it effortless," which aligns with their customer-first service approach.

The program has been extremely successful, with over 70% of employees either sending or receiving recognition and almost 100,000 e-cards being sent, which as a business having one third of their workforce working in the field, is no easy thing to achieve.

In addition to the program changing, the recognition culture itself has changed. An example is that in the past they had "Thank You Thursday" as a way to encourage employees to recognize one another, with over 15,000 e-cards being sent on one day. Now, recognition is so much a part of their culture that they've retired this initiative, with recognition happening every day of the week.

RECOGNITION PROGRAM

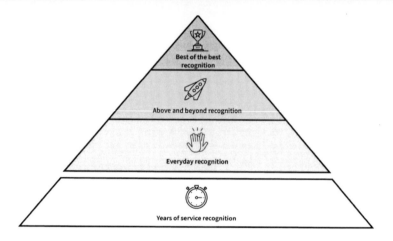

There are four levels and four individual plans in HomeServe's "STAR" recognition program:

 Anytime peer-to-peer e-cards: HomeServe has two types of e-cards that employees can send to one another at any time through their recognition platform. The first are e-cards that align with their values, and the second are Iso-greetings that connect employees with greetings such as "Little box of sunshine" or "Sending you a virtual hug."

In addition, e-cards are sent out to all employees from time to time to link to their diversity and inclusion strategy or align with holidays such as Valentine's Day to raise awareness and remind employees of the recognition platform.

"If you receive an eCard you are more likely to send one to a colleague, helping to drive our culture of recognition across the business and passing it on," says Roshine Bulpitt, Head of Engagement and Talent Development.

 "Shooting Star Awards" - anytime manager awards: All managers with five or more employees are given a budget to use for Shooting Star Awards, which can be sent at any time to reward their teams. Employees instantly receive £10 to spend on their discount platform, with no approval being required.

 "Shining Star Awards" - quarterly peer-to-peer nominated awards: To further encourage peer-to-peer recognition, HomeServe has their quarterly Shining Star Awards, which is when employees can nominate one another for going above and beyond when it comes to the customer, environment, colleagues or the business. There are 11 categories of awards, six representing their values plus additional ones such as "HomeServe Hero," "CEO Choice award," "Community Contributor" and "Career Developer."

Winners receive a cash award in the amount of £200 as well as a "money can't buy" experience such as a coaching from a member of the executive team, the ability to attend a meeting with an executive, or even a ride to work in a limousine or the Chief Exec's helicopter. "These are a way to do something invaluable to an employee's career or give them a once-in-a-lifetime experience," says Bulpitt.

 Years of service recognition: Employees receive service awards for every five years of service. They receive £100 to spend on their discounts platform, along with a certificate presented to them by their manager that has been signed by the CEO.

TIPS

- **Provide information to gain management support.**
  Get your managers and senior team onboard and behind
  your recognition programs by providing data and reports
  to support them to understand how they are using it and
  how they can do so even better.

- **Don't just put in a recognition program and then
  forget about it.** You need to keep communicating about
  it, reminding employees what it is and why it is important,
  driving them to your platform over and over again.

Hoxby Collective

COMPANY

Hoxby Collective (Hoxby) provides professional and creative services to a wide range of client organizations, from large global companies to small local startups. Their workforce is entirely remote and entirely freelance, enabling them to combine experts from around the world into diverse teams that are collectively more intelligent than traditional counterparts. Their mission is to "create a happier and more fulfilled society through a world of work without bias," which their workstyle model was created for – giving every person the complete freedom to choose when and where they work.

Hoxby has over 800 freelance members in more than 40 countries.

OVERVIEW

Hoxby's name is an acronym for "happiness of others multiplied by the best of you," and was built on the concept of a community – a community of freelance experts who harness their collective power to support their clients and one another professionally and personally. With no bricks, mortar or employment contracts to bind them, it was also built on the principle of reciprocity, doing so through shared values, behaviors and ways of working.

These concepts are brought to life through their recognition program, where genuine and meaningful exchanges of praise and gratitude are done freely across the community in their own unique way. Unique because it's uncommon to recognize freelancers, and unique because the recognition plans were designed inline with their values to bring them to life. This is true in the formal recognition plans that are shown in the next section, but also in plans such as their annual profit share, where

25% of profits are distributed to 100% of their members. This brings to life their value "#BetterTogether," signaling that results are achieved collectively by working together, with all members getting an equal portion of the profit regardless of the individual work they've done.

"Recognition has always been important for us since our talent comes from a freelance community that needs to be trusted to work together. We want to make every member feel valued and appreciated, building that trust and giving them a reason to stay and be a part of Hoxby," says Alex Hirst, Co-Founder and Joint CEO.

RECOGNITION PROGRAM

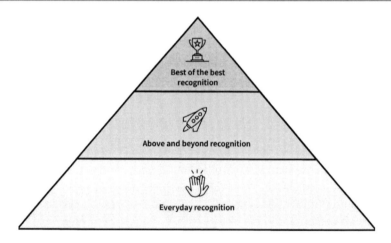

There are three levels and four individual plans in Hoxby's recognition program:

 "Hoxby Heroes" - weekly peer-to-peer recognition: Each week, members can nominate one another as their Hoxby Hero, recognizing them for embodying a value(s). There is no set number of nominations, with everyone who is nominated sharing in the limelight each week. There are always a number of different Hoxby Heroes each week, and in a model that relies on collective action, this is really important.

"HoxBox Surprise & Delight" - anytime peer-to-peer awards: Members can also recognize each other by sending a HoxBox, aimed at surprising and delighting one another. Whether to commemorate an anniversary, new baby or simply acknowledge a job well done, Hoxbies can request that a personalized gift box be sent to a fellow member of the Hoxby community at the click of a button. "The important thing is that we own the process to ensure that each package is personalized to the recipient, because it is in those details that we show that we genuinely care and understand each other that we build the foundations for collaboration," says Lizzie Penny, Co-Founder and Joint CEO.

"Hoxbies of Note Book" - anytime peer-to-peer recognition: Much like a chain letter, this recognition plan was started when one founder mailed a book to the other, writing on the first page to say just how brilliant they thought the other person was and with instructions to pass the book onto someone else. The other founder sent it forward with their own note of recognition, and so the practice began. Five years later, the book is still used as a way to recognize members of the community, being sent around the world from one member to another with new recognition messages to go alongside, and to be read, with those written over the years. There are basic instructions within the book that explain what to do and how to send it on to the next person, but the most important of them all is to keep the whole thing a secret. "We felt the real power of this book was its unexpected nature. It's a real treat to receive recognition in this way when so much of what we do is online," says Hirst.

"Hoxby Heroes" Awards" - annual peer-to-peer recognition: At the end of the year, they total up the number of Hoxby Hero weekly nominations and award the person with the most nominations with the Hoxby Hero of the Year Award. They also award the person who made the most nominations as their Hoxby Unsung Hero of the Year. In addition to the honor of receiving these awards, they receive one of the Surprise & Delight boxes.

TIPS

- **Recognition is personal and should therefore be individual.** At Hoxby, everything they do to recognize their people is done on an individual basis, whether it's naming them as a Hoxby Hero, sending them a HoxBox or the Hoxbies of Note Book.

- **Recognition is something you give and should therefore be proactive.** Whether it's nominating someone as a Hoxby Hero or suggesting they receive a HoxBox, it is the act of giving recognition that is a conscious choice and the proactivity of that can become a cultural norm.

InterGlobe Aviation Limited

COMPANY

InterGlobe Aviation Limited (IndiGo) is India's largest passenger airline with a market share of approximately 57%. They primarily operate in India's domestic air travel market as a low-cost carrier with a focus on their three pillars – offering low fares, being on time and delivering a courteous and hassle-free experience. Since their inception in August 2006, they've grown from a carrier with one plane to a fleet of 274, servicing 71 domestic destinations and 24 international ones.

IndiGo has approximately 25,000 employees located in India across domestic locations.

OVERVIEW

IndiGo's culture is called "3R," which stands for Respect all, Recognize efforts and contributions and Reward excellence. They are all ingrained in the design and delivery of their recognition framework, with each part having an important part to play in creating a culture where all employees feel valued and appreciated.

It begins with "Respect," which involves respecting the voice of their people, and can be seen in how they give their employees the opportunity to share ideas and provide feedback through "6E Speaks" (a pulse survey which is done every 15 days) and "6E Voice (a platform to share new ideas). It is also seen in the dedicated special days they have for different jobs, e.g. International Cabin Crew Day, Engineer's Day, Pilot's Day, Teacher's Day, etc. "These days make our people feel appreciated, knowing that they are important to the company. We encourage our workforce to go out and wish these employees a happy day, making it special for them," says Madhulika Chowdhary, Senior Manager, Talent Engagement.

It moves onto "Recognition" and "Reward," which involves the formal recognition given through the various recognition plans. They're all hosted on their mobile-app based internal social networking platform called "My 6E World," which makes recognition instant and hassle-free. Here, there are plenty of inspiring recognition stories being shared every day, showcasing the difference they've made to each other, the customer and the business. "Our business and our people have gone through some difficult times because of COVID-19, and we haven't been able to do a lot for them regarding their pay and benefits. Recognition has become even more important than it was in the past, being used as a way to let our people know that we appreciate their efforts and their hard work in many different ways," says Chowdhary.

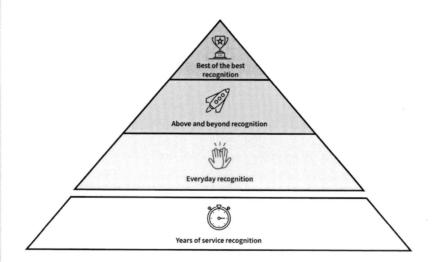

There are four levels and six individual plans in IndiGo's recognition program:

 "6E Claps" - anytime peer-to-peer e-cards: IndiGo's formal recognition program begins with their peer-to-peer recognition, which they call 6E Claps. Anyone can send an e-card through their digital platform, thanking and recognizing one another based on their values or a variety of other sentiments.

 "For Each Other" - anytime peer-to-peer awards: The next level is designed to help teams break down silos and encourage and strengthen intra-departmental partnerships through recognition. Once approved, points are awarded which the recipient can then redeem through their digital reward platform.

 Monthly/Quarterly/Annual department awards: The next level is awards that can be given for recognizing department-specific roles and contributions, with programs such as "6E Circle of Joy" and "6E Fighting Fit" to name a couple. Each department decides the timing and the amount of points to be awarded, and manages the approval and issuance of points to again be used through the platform.

 "6E Achievers Awards" - monthly people manager nominated awards: Every month, people managers from across the business can nominate employees and teams for 6E Achievers Awards. Between 20-30 winners are selected, with each receiving points that again can be spent on their reward platform.

 "Employee of the Quarter" - quarterly awards for operating teams: This award is for those employees who rise to the occasion and go beyond the call of duty to ensure the safety and wellbeing of IndiGo and its customers, dedicated to recognizing such shining stars and role models who are a testimony of the culture. The Chief Operating Officer reviews all of the monthly winners, and selects a winner from each function who receives a badge for their lanyard as well as points to be spent on their reward platform. In addition, a photograph of them is displayed on one of their aircrafts, with their family being invited for the unveiling, creating a great moment of pride for the employee, their family and their colleagues.

 Years of service recognition: All years of service are recognized at IndiGo by sending an e-card through their recognition platform. In addition, for milestone years (three, five, eight, 10, 12 and 15) they receive a special badge to put on their lanyard. And for 15 years, their blue lanyard is traded in for a yellow lanyard that says "IndiGo Legend."

TIPS

- **Consider combining formal and informal recognition programs as part of your strategy and approach**. These work together to deliver on your objectives and drive a recognition culture.

- **Recognition doesn't always have to be about the "big things."** It's just as important to create small but meaningful ways to appreciate one another for just being there for each other. An example was IndiGo's "happiness fiesta," where they held a variety of activities to connect their workforce and deliver happiness. One activity involved virtual happiness cloud badges that were developed on their digital platform, and which employees were instructed to give out to people who are part of their happiness cloud. "It was heartwarming to receive this badge from one another, and it was such a big hit that we're doing it again this year," says Chowdhary.

The Kellogg Company

COMPANY

The Kellogg Company (Kellogg's) is the world's leading producer of breakfast cereal and one of the biggest producers of snacks and convenience foods. Founded in 1894 by W.K. Kellogg who changed breakfast forever by creating Corn Flakes, Kellogg's has since fed the U.S. Army, gone to the moon, and now have a diverse portfolio of brands that are sold in over 180 countries, making everyday moments G-r-r-r-eat! Some of their well-loved brands include Special K®, Rice Krispies® and Pringles®.

Kellogg's has around 29,000 employees located in over 180 countries across the world.

OVERVIEW

About three years ago, Kellogg's European business launched their "Make it Happen" manifesto, which talked about being bold and courageous in how they think, act and deliver results. To go along with this, and to align with their value of "we love success," which talks about celebrating successes to make people feel valued and appreciated, the company also launched their new recognition program. This program has become an enabler of the new culture, helping it become a part of their DNA through recognizing and celebrating these new ways of working. As a result, the engagement score for "I regularly receive appropriate recognition when I do a good job" has increased by 11% since the launch.

But as with anything, this didn't just happen. Like their vision, which aspires to a world where "people are not just fed but fulfilled," they didn't just roll out a recognition platform, but have created a recognition culture where employees across the region are "fulfilled" by feeling valued and appreciated. Here are a few ways they've done this:

- **Recognition champions**: Since the launch of their recognition program, Kellogg's has had champions located across their sites. "These are the people who know what will work effectively at that location, role modeling, sponsoring, and walking the floor to get others involved," says Samantha Thomas-Berry, Vice President, European HR. "They are the passionate influencers that make recognition happen." Hand picked based on who best could fulfill this important role, and given training and support, these locally based people have truly made it happen and have made a difference.

- **Recognition campaigns**: Another thing Kellogg's has done is to have ad hoc campaigns throughout the year. As Thomas-Berry says, "By doing this it keeps recognition fresh, not samey, and happening on a regular basis." An example was a recent campaign linked to a wellbeing 5k challenge, where employees not only got involved with the activity, but also supported and recognized one another for achieving milestones and results through their recognition platform.

RECOGNITION PROGRAM

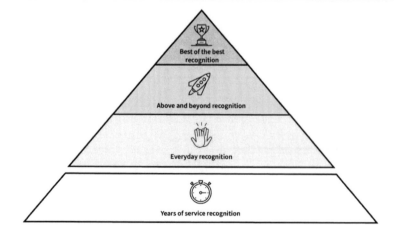

There are four levels and four individual plans in Kellogg's recognition program:

 Anytime peer-to-peer e-cards: Employees can recognize anyone at any time by sending a recognition e-card. They are based on their values, and are shared on the newsfeed for everyone to see and to reinforce by adding a like or a comment. In addition to these, e-cards are available to celebrate birthdays and other key milestones such as promotions.

 Anytime manager awards: The next level are awards that are given as points by managers at any time to recognize and reward their teams for going above and beyond and making a difference. They vary from 500 to 2,000 points ($5-20), which employees instantly receive to spend on their recognition platform, with no approval being required.

Points are allocated to managers each month, and if not spent by the end of the month, they are not carried over, but go away. "We used to carry them over but changed it as we want to encourage frequent recognition, with managers not holding off on recognizing important moments," says Thomas-Berry.

 "W.K. Kellogg Values Awards" - annual peer-to-peer nominated awards: The final level is the prestigious global W.K. Kellogg Values Awards, which are named after the founder of the company and celebrate the Kellogg's values. Once a year, employees can nominate one another for role modeling their values, with one individual or team winner selected within each region that is shortlisted by peers, and the winner selected by the leadership team.

All employees nominated are recognized in the recognition platform. The shortlist nominees receive a personalized letter from the area president and HR Director, along with points to spend on the recognition platform. The regional winner is invited to attend a celebration event at their headquarters in the U.S.

Here is what one winner posted in a blog to explain their experience at this event: "We were greeted by Tony the Tiger, enjoyed a dinner with company executives at Mr. Kellogg's former home and a large celebration where foods representing the international winner's home countries were prepared. Throughout our entire experience we were made to feel special, important and at home by our leaders and everyone at our headquarters. It was especially meaningful to have dinner with our Executive Committee and learn that they appreciated our hard work and wanted to understand how to best share our successes around the world."

 Years of service recognition: Employees receive service awards for every five years of service, being given the choice of a pin or points to spend on their recognition platform. In addition to these, employees receive an e-card to recognize and celebrate yearly anniversaries.

TIPS

- **Find ways to get people locally to own and champion recognition**. At Kellogg's this is done through their champions, who are their "passionate influencers" that create and drive a recognition culture.

- **When evolving your recognition program, make sure you're reviewing and evolving the awards that are given to reflect the shifting expectations of your employees**. At Kellogg's they've done this by offering choice between service pins and points, reflecting that pins are no longer for everyone, carrying the symbolism that they did in the past.

Kentucky Fried Chicken

COMPANY

COMPANY

Kentucky Fried Chicken (KFC) is a global fast food restaurant chain that specializes in fried chicken, and is part of the Yum! Brand. Besides having a passion for food, they're also passionate about making a positive social and environmental impact, helping people get a foot on the work ladder, caring for their communities and offering balanced food choices. As they say, "There's more Behind the Bucket than you think."

In the UK and Ireland, KFC has 30,000 employees as part of their franchise of 1,000 owner-operated restaurants as well as in their head office.

OVERVIEW

Recognition is at the core and at the heart of the KFC culture, as evidenced in the fact that one of their organizational values is "recognize, recognize, recognize." According to Neil Piper, Chief People Officer, "Recognition is a constant drum beat of our culture, something that differentiates us and something that we are passionate about. We believe in recognizing the brilliance in our people, focusing on the simple thank yous and the power of personal connections through recognition."

KFC's recognition program reflects and supports the diversity of their team, and the joy they have in recognizing one another. This is seen in the personalized awards that employees are encouraged to give based on their hobbies, interests, and passions. Two examples are ones that Piper gives out – His "Culture Vulture" award, which is a £3.99 (things don't have to cost a lot to make a difference!) squeaky vulture dog toy, and is given for bringing the KFC culture to life. And his "Here's to You" award, which is a book that is a collection of quotes about traits of wonderful humans, with Piper selecting the one that best fits what he is recognizing the person for, adding a handwritten note to personalize it further.

"Because we encourage everyone to come up with their own awards, we end up with a random collection of them. And although they may not be all shiny, they each have meaning to the person giving them, creating a connection, and driving a genuine and authentic recognition culture," says Piper.

To further drive this recognition culture, one of KFC's leadership competencies is about creating a sense of recognition. Leaders are assessed against this, being done through employee surveys that are run every eight weeks in their restaurants. "Recognition should never be a mandate, but if you can land an authentic, well-intended culture of recognition then it can become a positive expectation, and is considered as a part of doing a good job as a leader," says Piper.

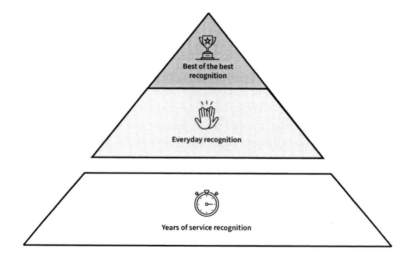

RECOGNITION PROGRAM

- Best of the best recognition
- Everyday recognition
- Years of service recognition

There are three levels and four individual plans in KFC's recognition program:

 Anytime peer-to-peer e-cards and virtual badges: This is the newest of KFC's recognition programs, launching in 2022. On the digital platform, employees are able to recognize one another at any point in time for demonstrating their values and behaviors, awarding digital badges that can be traded in for company swag and other recognition gifts. This virtual platform sits as part of an internally facing KFC App, a virtual World for their 30,000 team members to access the information and the community they need to thrive as a part of Team KFC.

 Anytime peer-to-peer personalized recognition gifts: At the same level in the recognition pyramid are personalized recognition gifts, which again can be given by anyone at any time to reflect everyday appreciation. As described earlier, this is where employees come up with their own unique and creative awards to give out to recognize one another.

 "Champions Club" - annual awards: For restaurants, KFC has their annual Champions Club, which is awarded to the top restaurants based off of a balanced scorecard. In addition, they also celebrate and award others for achievements such as giving back to the community, leading with heart, growing and developing their people or doing the right thing for their customer. All winners are invited to an awards event spanning three days that is full of amazing experiences, and also receive exclusive branded merchandise and luxury gifts of their choice.

 Years of service recognition: Employees receive service awards for every five years of service. They receive commemorative plaques and personal gifts allowances increasing in value as the length of service does.

TIPS

- **Never underestimate the power of authentic recognition and the difference it can make to your workforce.** Especially at a company like KFC where such a large percentage of their workforce are young and new to the workplace, recognition can act as a confidence builder, as a way to improve their self esteem and make them feel a sense of belonging.

- **Look for opportunities to bring personalization into recognition.** Let your people recognize in ways that are right for them, either in words or actions, so that they can deliver recognition in a more meaningful and authentic way.

Key Forensic Services

Key Forensic Services (KFS) is one of the leading forensic science providers in the U.K. and Europe, offering a full range of forensic services to the criminal justice system, defense lawyers and private sector companies.

KFS has over 270 employees located across four strategically placed sites in the U.K. – Coventry, Bristol, Norwich and Warrington.

When HR Director Janet Hulme joined KFS, there was no formal approach to recognition. Teams were given commendations from the police force for work they did to support solving cases from time to time, but that was about it. Hulme then went around the sites and held focus groups, finding out what kind of recognition her employees wanted and needed. Using this, they created their recognition program, launching it in a phased approach. "We didn't want to hit everybody with everything at the same time, we wanted to phase it in, maintaining interest and anticipation of what was to come next," says Hulme.

They initially launched e-cards on Valentine's Day 2020 on their digital recognition platform, doing so on this day to show from the beginning that the company appreciated them. This campaign, and all of the others, were done as teaser campaigns, building up excitement as they shared small clues as to what was coming next.

Besides their formal recognition program, they also have a calendar of events they use to plan Staff Appreciation and Wellbeing Days throughout the year. Anything from National

Chocolate Day to Eat a Red Apple Day, they use this as an opportunity to have a bit of fun, and at the same time, recognize their workforce. "The work we do can be hard and harrowing, so we use this as a way to show our people that we appreciate the great work they are doing," says Hulme.

A recent example was a campaign they did on National Fish & Chips Day, where vans turned up at each site to deliver the pre-chosen food employees had ordered. "It created such a buzz and actually led to productivity increasing by 28% on that day, compared to the same day in previous weeks," says Hulme. This could have been because of the chemicals released from recognition or those from the fish, but either way, it was a great result!

RECOGNITION PROGRAM

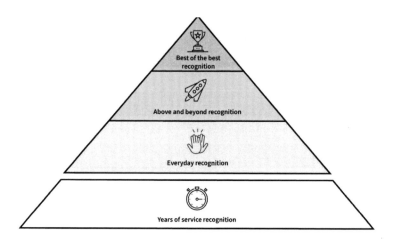

There are four levels and five individual plans in KFS's recognition program:

 Anytime peer-to-peer e-cards: KFS has two types of e-cards that employees can send to one another at any time through their recognition platform. The first are e-cards that align with their values, and the second are general greetings. An example of a general greeting is one that welcomes new employees to the company, which as an added bonus introduces them to the digital recognition platform, and sends the message from the start that recognition is a key part of their culture and ways of working

During the pandemic they had special e-cards designed to support their employees, who were classed as essential workers, and thus had to come to work during the various lockdowns. Examples of these are ones that said "Not all heroes wear capes" and "Essential doesn't cover it."

 Anytime manager postcards and gifts: To add to and supplement anytime recognition, they launched a recognition plan that managers can use to recognize higher level contributions. These are physical postcards managers can give out instantly on an ad hoc basis, accompanying them with a gift valued at £5 that managers buy based on what they believe the employee would like. "We do this outside of the digital recognition platform as we wanted to give out something physical. Everyone deals with so much technology, we thought this would create a different reaction and feeling," says Hulme.

 Monthly peer-to-peer nominated awards: The next level of recognition was added three months after the introduction of e-cards, and is their employee of the month awards. This plan was developed in response to suggestions from their Staff Representatives, and is linked to a former employee named Emma White who passed away. They recognize employees who embody the behaviors and values extolled by her, going above what their peers expect of them in their roles and other related duties beyond their own in an effort to make the company more effective and a great place to work for all. Employees can nominate one another each month for this award, with a director at their parent company selecting the winner so that it's done in an impartial way. The names of all employees nominated appear in a monthly blog along with the name of the winner who also receives a call from either the HR Director or their line manager to congratulate them, along with a £50 voucher to use on their discount platform and a handwritten certificate.

 "Emma White Award" - annual peer-to-peer nominated award: The top level of recognition is the Emma White Award, which as with the previous award, is linked to their former employee Emma White. All monthly winners are eligible, with one person selected by the same person selecting monthly winners. The winner receives a £500 cash award, a certificate, and a gift of flowers, chocolates or alcohol based on their personal preference. Additionally, a blog is published about them on their intranet with the winner's permission.

 Years of service recognition: They celebrate every year of service at KFS by sending an anniversary e-card from their recognition platform. For every five years of service, employees receive an additional day of annual leave to take that year and a handwritten certificate. For 10 years and above they also receive a gift – at 10 years it's a £50 voucher to use on their discount platform, at 15 years it's a meal with family or friends up to the value of £150, and at 20 years it's a weekend getaway with a partner or friend up to value of £300. These awards intentionally blend time off, money and experiences to celebrate years of service in a variety of ways.

TIPS

- **Look at ways to multiply the impact of recognition by creating different elements and/or touchpoints.** For example, at KFS they do this with the Employee of the Month awards by winners receiving a certificate, a phone call, a voucher and their name in a blog. Together, they create a more meaningful and lasting impression.

- **Consider staggering the launch of your individual recognition plans.** This helps create a greater impact with each one individually, and keeps the excitement, interest and engagement with them as time goes on.

KP Snacks

Started in 1853 selling jam, and in 1948 becoming one of the first companies in the U.K. to sell potato chips, KP Snacks (KP) is now one of the fastest growing snack businesses in the U.K. They manufacture some of the most iconic British brands including McCoy's™, Hula-Hoops™, Butterkist™, Pom-Bear™ and Tyrrells™.

KP has over 2,200 colleagues across seven factories around the U.K. and their contemporary head office.

OVERVIEW

As a company that has a purpose statement of "creating happy snacking moments," it should be no surprise that KP has put a focus on creating not just happy moments for their customers through their products, but also for their employees through recognition. And just like products which have evolved over the years, so too has their recognition program, moving from a traditional hierarchical approach to one that drives everyday recognition to recognize the efforts, behaviors and outputs of each and every colleague to make them feel valued and appreciated.

Another part of their evolution has been a change from simple notes used by one team, to a fully online recognition program that's used across the business. Here are the four parts of this evolution which you may find interesting as you evolve your program:

1. **Handwritten notes**: Recognition began with handwritten notes which the Marketing team started using when their new values were launched. They'd write each other notes which they'd put on each other's desks to celebrate living these

values. So when the values champion for Marketing shared this great idea with the rest of the team, they decided to create something to be used for the entire office.

2. **Call out cards**: The team then developed "Call out cards," which are postcards used across the entire office to recognize, or call out, someone living a value. Colleagues would write each other postcards, put them in a post box in the office, and then they were handed out to recipients once a week. In addition, each week one of the champions wrote a Feel Good Friday email which listed everyone who had been called out that week.

3. **Google form**: The team decided that this wasn't enough, that they wanted the option to call out people based in other KP locations, so they next developed a Google form that could be used in this way.

4. **Online e-cards**: However, as the number of recognition moments increased they realized that they needed something more robust, so the team then put in place an online recognition program. Employees across the entire business can now recognize one another by sending e-cards using a digital recognition platform, supporting and driving a strong recognition culture. Since the start of 2021, over 2,000 e-cards are sent every month and everyone can see them as they happen in real time via the App which gives the added benefit for people to like or add comments to endorse them. The Friday email still happens, however with some Excel wizardry this has become a lot easier to do.

"We have completely evolved recognition and what we recognize. We used to give lavish prizes to a few people who had achieved something over and above expectations. As we built capability and became more successful, the above and beyond became the norm. Now we have a system that encourages instant, every day recognition between peers that reaches so many more people, and by linking it to our values and behaviors we have achieved many more amazing results for the business," says Johanna Dickinson, HR Director.

RECOGNITION PROGRAM

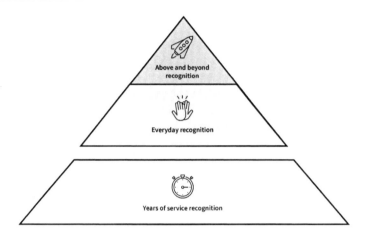

There are three levels and three individual plans in KP's recognition program:

 "Call Outs" - anytime peer-to-peer e-cards: A core part of KP's recognition program are their Call Out e-cards, which can be sent by anyone at any time, and can be shared on their virtual social recognition wall.

To multiply the impact and visibility of Call Outs, they also have a practice called "Feel Good Friday," which is a weekly email that shares the names of all Call Out recipients. "We wanted to make sure that everyone knew about the recognition taking place, celebrating them, and also calling out positive behaviours to be repeated," says Dickinson.

 Discretionary functional/site awards: The next level are discretionary financial awards that can be awarded by line managers, the executive leadership team or functional heads to individuals or teams. The criteria for them is going above and beyond in the demonstration of their values and behaviors in their day-to-day role, activity or project. At the discretion of the management team, employees can receive between £20 and £200 based on their contributions, which is put into the employee's KP4ME online employee discount account where they can spend the money any way they wish.

"We moved to this approach recently as we wanted to stop functions and sites buying things ad hoc through expenses. Instead, we wanted something that would be done in a consistent way that we can report on and measure, and also help our employees' money go further through the discount platform," says Dickinson.

 Years of service recognition: Another element that is managed at the function/site level are KP's years of service recognition. Again, the local management team decide the amount to be awarded within the KP4ME discount platform, and also on how to celebrate the anniversary.

One example is a manufacturing site who has created a "tree of life" that shows a leaf for every employee, with different years of service being a different color and appearing at a different height depending on how long they've been at the company.

TIPS

- **Understand what your people value when it comes to recognition**. For example, KP's recognition program was developed from continually listening to what their people wanted, evolving it as their needs changed.

- **Go back and review your recognition programs over and over again.** You can do this by conducting a health check to ensure that your program is doing what you designed it to do.

LinkedIn

COMPANY

LinkedIn began in Co-founder Reid Hoffman's living room in 2002 and was officially launched on May 5, 2003. Today, they are the world's largest professional network on the Internet with 774+ million members in more than 200 countries and territories worldwide. People use the tool to find the right job or internship, connect and strengthen professional relationships and learn skills to help them succeed in their career.

LinkedIn has over 16,000 employees located across more than 20 countries.

OVERVIEW

LinkedIn's global recognition program represents the journey they've been on to design and evolve one that aligns with their culture, and keeps pace with how the company and the world have and continue to change. "Our program clears the runway for what we want our business and people to achieve. It's been a natural evolution of where we are and where we want to be," says Katherine Gilbert, Senior Director, Compensation & Benefits EMEA/LatAm.

An example is "Bravo! Distinguish," an industry-leading new element of their Bravo! recognition program that launched in July 2021. Put in place to support and drive their commitment to DIBS (diversity, inclusion and belonging), it mirrors and sits alongside the existing recognition program as a way to recognize the important work their 500 global employee volunteers do on top of their day jobs to support this important initiative.

Another example is "award advisor," something they've built into their recognition system to drive a sense of fairness and equity in how recognition awards are determined and granted. The award advisor appears in the system any time an employee makes a recognition nomination, asking a series of questions to assist and guide the employee to the most appropriate award based on the scope and impact of the contributions. "In the past this was an optional step in the process, but we've made it mandatory to ensure consistency and to remove as much unconscious bias as possible," says Gilbert.

All of these efforts are paying off, and according to Gilbert 94% of their global workforce is recognized each year, with a recognition moment occurring every five minutes!

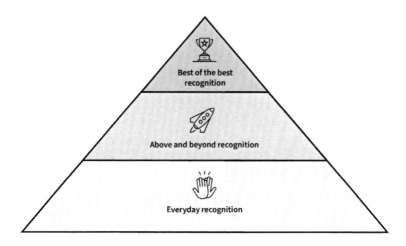

There are three levels in LinkedIn's global "Bravo!" recognition program:

 "Thanks" - anytime peer-to-peer e-cards: The first level is e-cards, which they call Thanks. They can be sent by anyone at any time to acknowledge one another for exhibiting the behaviors and demonstrating the core culture and values of the company.

"Shout Out, Cheers, Applause, Limelight, Spotlight & Distinguish Awards" - anytime peer-to-peer awards: The next level is the five points-based awards along with the Distinguish Awards, which as previously mentioned recognizes contributions in respect to DIBS. Employees can nominate one another for these, with differing levels of approval required based on the point value, but all done "in the moment" so that employees do not need to wait to be recognized.

The awards are intended to acknowledge and reward colleagues for going above and beyond by putting forth exceptional effort, going beyond what is expected or producing outstanding results. As mentioned previously, there is a tool called "award advisor" that helps employees determine the appropriate award level based on the behaviors and actions demonstrated against their core values.

 "Ovation, Rave, Encore & Distinguish Awards" - anytime peer-to-peer cash awards: The final level is the three cash-based awards along with the Distinguish Awards. These run similarly to the points-based awards in that anyone can nominate anyone, approval is required, and the award advisor assists them but they reflect higher levels of overall contribution and impact.

TIPS

- **Don't let a system drive the design of your program.** For example, at LinkedIn they found that because each manager's recognition budget had to balance the contributions made through the DIBS work along with everything else, there was not enough being used to recognize the contributions made in this important area. For this reason, and as mentioned earlier, they created a standalone element of their recognition program, Bravo! Distinguish, so that both elements of recognition would get the focus, attention, and reward and recognition they both deserved, not letting the system hurdles get in the way.

- **Always look through the data and analytical lens when reviewing your program.** For example, at LinkedIn they found by analyzing their data they were missing a recognition award "sweet spot" as Gilbert called it, as awards jumped from $30 to $150, and actions showed that they needed something in between to reflect the most appropriate levels of contribution. By adding in an award at $75 it did just this, and it's now the most used award level.

"We look at data every which way we can to look for opportunities to improve our program or to see what else needs to be done. We make the connections and we connect the data dots to make sure that our recognition program does what it 'says on the tin' to drive our business and foster our culture – which we believe is a real differentiator for us," says Gilbert.

Missguided

Missguided is one of the fastest growing women's online retailers in the world, selling to customers in over 180 countries. Founded in 2009 in the U.K. by Nitin Passi, their mission is to empower women by inspiring self-confidence in mind, body and potential. Missguided is built on an agile model to deliver affordable, quality products, the latest trending styles, and unexpected brand collaborations to customers across the globe.

Missguided has 400 employees who are based in their office in Manchester, England.

OVERVIEW

Creating an engaging work life is important at Missguided – from an exciting work environment (yes, they do have a selfie tunnel and a learning loft!), to an extraordinary and unique approach to recognition which can best be described as authentic and organic. Authentic, because it genuinely reflects and resonates with their demographics, and organic because it's constantly reviewed and updated to reflect the needs of the business, their people, and what's going on in the world in general. "We don't want recognition to be stagnant or it becomes like wallpaper, it constantly needs to be elevated and kept fresh. That's why we drop things in and out, recognizing for the same behaviors and actions, but doing so in different ways. And if it doesn't work, we scrap it!" says Glenn Grayson, Internal Communications & Engagement Partner.

Here are three examples of how Missguided has done this:

- Created a recognition campaign called "Yellow Monday" to change the color and feelings associated with Mondays, sending messages of positivity to start the week out right. They did this by creating branded e-cards, and randomly selecting winners from those who sent e-cards, rewarding them with a voucher for a free coffee.

- Moved to use their e-cards to share positivity outside of the company, linking in with causes and communities their colleagues say matter to them. For example, during Pride Month, a donation to a LGBT+ charity was made for every e-card that was sent, and for World Kindness Day they donated to a local food bank for e-cards sent.

- When noticing a drop in nominations for their monthly "Vibe Awards," they rephrased how they announced it in their newsletter from focusing on "nominating the person who lives our vibes (values)" to "nominating someone to receive a £100 voucher." This change worked like a charm, increasing nominations from only two in the previous month to 36 the following month.

RECOGNITION PROGRAM

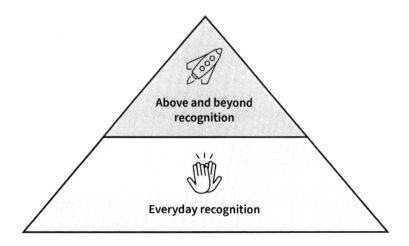

There are two levels and three individual plans in Missguided's recognition program:

 Anytime peer-to-peer e-cards: e-cards are available on Missguided's recognition platform, and can be sent by anyone at any time. They align with their diversity and inclusion strategy, having a wide variety available that include those for all religious holidays. In addition, they have e-cards for what Grayson calls "general sorts of feelings," which are unique to their culture, and include messages such as "You Give Me Life," "You're Stronger Than You Think," "Totally Appreciate You," "Miss Your Face" and "Frickin' Awesome." "Our e-cards are intended to be fun and engaging, using language that our employees are accustomed to, getting the right balance for our workforce," says Grayson.

98% of the workforce either sent or received e-cards, showing how they have been effective in creating and driving a culture of recognition.

 Anytime peer-to-peer postcards: Postcards are where recognition began at Missguided, with a celebration station set up on each floor that contained recognition postcards similar to what you'd find at a greeting card store. They are so much a part of their recognition culture, that even with the setup of e-cards, they continue to use postcards as another way to recognize one another. New employees are given a set of these postcards in their new starter swag bag, and during their induction are instructed to give one out to someone who has helped make their first week special, helping them begin their recognition journey at the company.

 "Vibe Awards" - monthly peer-to-peer nominated awards: Vibe Awards were created to recognize employees for living the company's values, or what Missgided call "vibes." Employees can nominate colleagues each month for one of these awards, and their values ambassadors select two winners who receive a £100 shopping voucher.

The program was launched during the pandemic, so instead

of surprising winners in person, they first sent balloons to their homes, and then moved to sending confetti cube cards that turn into a trophy showcasing their values and letting them know that they were a winner. "We did this because we wanted to have a bit of fun and have a surprise element, putting a smile on their faces," says Grayson.

TIPS

- **Make sure that your program is authentic to your business, brand and culture.** What's right for one company may not be right for you.

- **Be open, honest and transparent.** Explain every detail of how your program works, such as explaining how winners are selected, so they are perceived to be fair and consistent.

- **Don't be afraid to change things.** Always keep your program relevant and fresh.

NAHL Group plc

COMPANY

NAHL Group plc (NAHL) is the parent company of National Accident Law (comprising the National Accident Helpline brand), Homeward Legal, Searches UK (Searches) and Bush & Company Rehabilitation (Bush & Co). Founded in 1993, they leverage the strength of their brand, technology and processes to provide exceptional service to their customers by being outstanding in everything they do.

NAHL has over 200 employees working in their three offices across the East Midlands and the South East of England.

OVERVIEW

NAHL's recognition program can be summed up in one word – evolving. When I interviewed them for one of my previous books, they explained how they'd evolved from a program centered around long service awards to one centered around their new company values, putting in place programs such as "Value Heroes," "Value Stars" and "CEO Stars." But when I interviewed them again for this book, they explained how they'd evolved yet again, replacing these programs with new ones that better meet the changing needs of their business and their people.

"In 2020 in the middle of the pandemic when business was tough, we made the decision to remove our financially-based recognition awards. We decided to focus on 'heartfelt recognition,' the words and not the gifts. Our people understood why we did this, they don't seem to miss it, and if anything recognition has become better than it ever was in the past with 80% saying they feel recognized," says Marcus Lamont, Group HR Director.

In addition to evolving their recognition program, they've also evolved their approach to recognition in these two ways:

- Training: They've put in place robust training to ensure that each and every employee understands not just how to recognize, but why it's important and the difference it can make to the business and to each other.

- Recognize the recognizer: They've moved to layer on recognizing individuals who recognize others, sending a "hug" from time-to-time to this person to show them that they are appreciated for their recognition actions and the difference they're making.

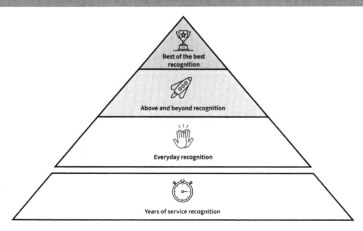

RECOGNITION PROGRAM

There are four levels and four individual plans in NAHL's recognition program:

 "Kudos" - anytime peer-to-peer e-cards: Their recognition program starts out with Kudos, which are e-cards based on their five company values. They can be sent by anyone at any time through their recognition platform, and help drive a culture of continuous and meaningful recognition. Managers are targeted to use all 20 kudos credits as regularly as possible, with a goal to recognize every employee, every seven days.

"Teamie of the Month" - monthly peer-to-peer nominated awards: These awards take place every month, with employees nominating one another for Teamie of the Month, aligning with their value of being "unified." Responsibility for the process changes each month, with a different member of each team reviewing all nominations, selecting and announcing the winner, as well as reading out all nominations during the monthly team meeting so that everyone can hear the kind words being said about each other. The winner receives no financial award, but has the honor of being selected as team member of the month.

 Annual peer-to-peer nominated awards: The final program is their annual awards, where employees nominate one another for awards such as values champions, employee's choice award, team of year, manager of the year, etc. Winners are announced at their annual event, which is attended by all employees and their partners.

Team and manager of the year winners receive a night out together as a team, and the employee's choice winner receives a weekend away. Values champion winners receive £150 to spend on their own development, along with the responsibility of representing their division in their annual employee survey by presenting it to their team and then gathering feedback on specific actions.

"It's a great development opportunity for our values champions, not just through the money they receive for their personal development, but in owning and taking responsibility for improving employee engagement through the employee survey. We support them by training them so that they can take on this important role," says Lamont.

 Years of service recognition: These awards introduce the concept of "surprise" into their recognition program, as employees who reach five, 10, 15 and 20 years of service are surprised by a special gift selected just for them.

"We search on social media to find out what the employee is interested in, and select a gift that is personal to them. From a specific book they've always wanted to read, to an activity they've spoken about, we surprise them with this personal and heartfelt touch to show them that they are appreciated and valued," says Lamont.

TIPS

- **Constantly review and evolve your recognition program, making sure it meets the changing needs of your business and your people.** NAHL has done this multiple times in removing, adding and changing their programs, keeping them fresh and current.

- **Find ways to integrate the element of surprise into your recognition program.** NAHL has done this with personalizing long service awards, the drama in selecting winners for their monthly and annual awards and by surprising employees as they change their recognition programs.

Nationwide

COMPANY

Nationwide is the world's largest building society, run for the benefit of their 15 million members. As a mutual organization, Nationwide is guided by a social purpose which they interpret as "building society, nationwide." Nationwide's mission is to "work hard every day to meet the insurance and financial needs of our customers, at every stage of life."

Nationwide has approximately 18,000 employees, located across the U.K.

OVERVIEW

When the team at Nationwide decided to review their recognition proposition, they knew it was strong, but felt the impact was being limited due to fragmented processes and systems, inconsistent experiences across the Society and a lack of awareness of the different offerings within the proposition. As a result, they did a deep dive into the program, bringing in design-thinking methodology to map out and design a new cohesive and effective recognition experience. They did this by following these key steps:

- Carried out in-depth research through interviews, surveys and focus groups to understand their employees' pain points and challenges.

- Ran ideation sessions to generate and develop ideas, co-designing new solutions.

- Prototyped and tested future experiences with a group of employees to refine concepts and capture new ideas.

"We wanted to enhance our recognition proposition so that it fosters an environment where more of our people feel valued for their personal and team contribution, motivating best performance and promoting the mutual behaviors that underpin how we do business differently," says Alissa Davis, Head of Reward & Benefits.

Since its launch in February 2021, Nationwide's revamped recognition program has really taken off, and they're seeing more recognition than ever before with over 75% of their total workforce, including contingent workers, engaging with it.

RECOGNITION PROGRAM

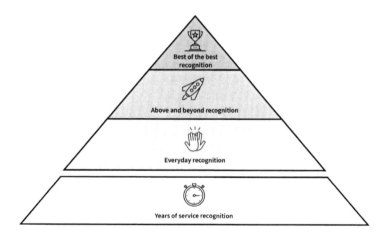

There are four levels and four individual plans in Nationwide's "Appreciate" recognition program:

 Anytime peer-to-peer e-cards: Nationwide's e-cards are built around three categories - values, support (e.g. being a LGBTQ+ ally, being an advocate of gender equality), and moments that matter (e.g. birthdays, anniversaries, welcome to the team).

When they were launched, the numbers surpassed their expectations, with over 80,000 being sent out in just four months. This was due to the e-cards being more engaging and clearly defined, being more visible through their social recognition wall, being accessed now through single sign-on and an app, and with an innovative communications campaign that included webcasts, radio interviews, custom recognition GIFs, and even the creation of a special recognition poem.

 Anytime peer-to-peer awards: These awards can be sent by any employee at any time through their recognition platform. Two changes were made to this program. First, the level of approval was pushed lower so that recognition could happen quicker, with only line manager approval required. Second, to help employees and managers decide the appropriate award amount, a table was developed to provide examples of the types of actions and behaviors at each award level, as well as what an employee could do with the award (e.g. a £25 award could be used to buy a voucher for their favorite retailer).

 Annual peer-to-peer nominated awards: Once a year, employees can nominate one another to receive an award, with award types changing year to year based on what is relevant. Some of the new ones added for 2021 were the "Mutual Respect" award, which is aligned with their diversity and inclusion strategy, the "Unsung Hero" award to recognize those who do great things under the radar and the "Fresh Perspective" award to recognize newcomers. Winners receive a cash award as well as an invitation to their annual awards dinner.

 Years of service recognition: Nationwide has industry-leading retention, and thus recognizes long service at one, five, 10, 20, 30, 40 and 50 years. As part of the review, the focus of the awards was changed to be less about money, and more about creating a sense of celebration and making it memorable. They did this by decreasing the financial awards, and increasing the amount of time off given. In addition, they added e-cards on their platform for all years of service which managers could send, share on the social recognition wall and celebrate together.

TIPS

- **Invest the time upfront understanding and mapping out the entire recognition experience and journey.** Build these findings into both the design and delivery of recognition moments. At Nationwide, they created a recognition playbook to map out these key moments in detail, which was then shared with their new recognition provider to make it a seamless integration process.

- **Focus your initial communications on the why.** Always explain your why (why recognition is important), and not just the what (how to use the recognition program) in order to win the hearts and minds of your people.

NextLevel Internet

COMPANY

NextLevel Internet (NextLevel) is a cloud-based voice, internet and unified communication service provider that was founded in 1999. They work with their clients to provide a flexible, cost-effective unified communication service, helping to create the ideal workplace, where business can be done more efficiently and effectively.

They have about 50 employees, located in three locations across the U.S.

OVERVIEW

NextLevel's approach to recognition is one that is intentional – intentional in how they focus on the whole person, and intentional in how they focus on delivering moments of joy. This was clear from the start when I interviewed Patti Cuthill, Chief Joy Officer, who began explaining their recognition program by sharing a story of how the company came together to support an employee's sick child, and how each employees' words of encouragement were woven into a quilt along with pictures of her family and favorite things. Is this traditional recognition? No. Is this meaningful and important? Absolutely. "We are trying to build a connection with our people, showing appreciation and celebrating with them in the good times and being there for them in the difficult ones. It's all connected," says Cuthill.

Another example is their approach to delivering recognition early in the employee lifecycle. During the interview process, each candidate that makes it to the final interview stage, regardless of whether they get the job, receives a little care package to thank them for taking the time to interview with them. During the new hire process, once a job is offered and accepted, they are sent a personalized welcome video from Cuthill along with one from their new team. And on their first day of work, they are taken out to lunch by NextLevel's President. "We set the tone and send a message from the start as to how they'll be cared for, valued and appreciated," says Cuthill.

And finally, another example is with their approach to understanding and identifying recognition that is right for the individual. This is done by having each employee take a "Motivating by Appreciation" assessment to identify how best to appreciate them in ways that are meaningful and "hit the mark" for the person. In addition, employees can add any of their personal preferences, ensuring that recognition truly delivers those moments of joy.

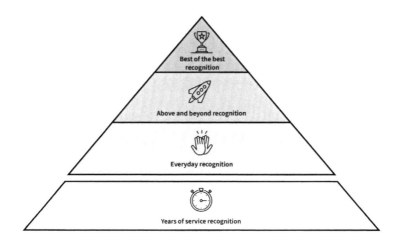

There are four levels and five individual plans in NextLevel's recognition program:

 "High Fives" - anytime peer-to-peer eCards: The first level of recognition is their High Fives, which can be sent at any time to anyone through their social recognition platform and are based on demonstrating their company values. To go along with these, and to magnify the recognition moments, during their Friday team huddles, the President reads out the recognition messages, celebrating them for a second time.

 "A Night on the Town Awards" - anytime rewards: The next level is given for going above and beyond, or what Cuthill describes as discretionary effort that is "loud and proud." They can be given at any time by a leader, with winners being given a crisp $100 bill that they can use to go out on the town and celebrate with their family and friends. This is the only financial award, however, it's not really about the money, as it's about the experience of a celebratory moment.

 "Legendary Service Awards" - quarterly peer-to-peer nominated awards: The next level is awarded for demonstrating exemplary client service, and is based around Ken Blanchard's "Legendary Service" model. Each quarter employees nominate one another for consistently delivering against these service standards, with Cuthill and the President selecting the winners who win a special cube that has their name engraved on it.

 "The Greater Good Awards" - quarterly awards: The other part of the quarterly awards is based on their value of "the greater good," which talks about serving the community. Each quarter, one person is selected to receive the award based on their involvement in the community through volunteering, and is given $3,000 to donate to their chosen charity.

 Years of service recognition: Each year, NextLevel recognizes their employees for their time with the company. From a $50 gift card, to flowers or something else, the People & Culture Team selects a special treat just for them.

TIPS

- **Look for appreciation and recognition moments everywhere.** There's no limit to where you can find opportunities to recognize, so look for them in every part of the employee experience and in every part of your people's lives.

- **Focus recognition on appreciating the behaviors that have been demonstrated and not on the reward that is being given.** "You shouldn't have to tie everything to money, your employees should take pride in their great work and for your appreciation of their efforts," says Cuthill.

North Construction & Building

COMPANY

Founded in 1987, North Construction & Building (North) is an Australian-based construction company that works across a diverse range of projects within the commercial, education, aged care, health, industrial, infrastructure, retail and hospitality sectors. From fit-out and refurbishments through to greenfield developments, they have an award-winning reputation for excellence.

North has around 100 employees located across five offices and 20 construction sites throughout Australia.

OVERVIEW

North is, and has always been, a values-based business, with their five values driving their business, their people and their culture. These values also drive their recognition program, which over the years has been carefully crafted to put the spotlight on these values, recognizing and rewarding achievements that link to and promote them. "By doing this we make sure that our values are front and center, strengthening their understanding and the impact they have," says Matthew Cook, Managing Director.

One value that has directly influenced the design of their recognition program is "excellence," which focuses on the relentless pursuit of improvement, acknowledging the need to learn and improve incrementally. By recognizing and celebrating these incremental successes, and not just the big wins, it ensures an emphasis on innovation, efficiency and practicality.

RECOGNITION PROGRAM

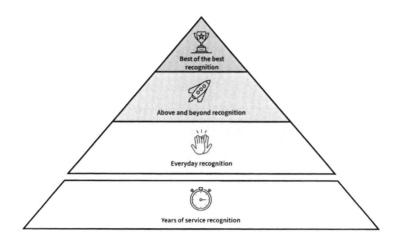

There are four levels and six individual plans in North's recognition program:

 "Cheers Peers" anytime peer-to-peer e-cards: The starting point for recognition at North is their values-based e-cards, called Cheers Peers, that are available on their recognition platform. They can be sent by anyone at any time, and can be shared on their virtual, social recognition wall. In addition to these, other e-cards are available to celebrate key milestones such as birthdays, the birth of a child, weddings and engagements.

 "Icing on the Cake" birthday awards: To celebrate and recognize birthdays, all employees receive the special birthday e-card as mentioned above, as well as $25 AUD into their recognition account, which they can spend as they wish.

 "True North Awards" - anytime peer-to-peer awards: The next level is True North Awards, which can be sent by any employee at any time to recognize a colleague for going above and beyond to truly align with their values. There is no limit to how many of these awards can be given, although they are uploaded into the system on a quarterly basis to ensure unallocated balances do not simply go unused. No approval is required for them to be sent, and recipients receive $25 AUD into their recognition account.

 "Ambassador Awards" - anytime Ambassador given awards: The next level is the Ambassador Awards, which can be given to any individual or team at any point in time by North's Ambassadors, a group of passionate and highly engaged employees who sit across the organization to promote and drive their various engagement programs. As explained on their recognition platform, "Our Ambassadors are always on the lookout for peers who are actively applying our values into their attitude, work ethics and projects – remaining positive through the tough times, aspiring to be your best, and supporting your teammates."

The Ambassadors can give out eight of these awards a year, however this number can be increased if necessary. There is no approval required for them to be sent, and like the previous level, recipients receive $25 AUD into their recognition account.

 "Northie Awards" - monthly senior management awards: The top level of recognition is the Northie Awards, inspired by founder Michael North, and awarded for exceptional work ethics, excellence in performance and for being a positive role model for others in the business. These awards are given out by senior management, who each month come together to select the winners, awarding them $250 AUD to be put into their recognition account.

There is no magic number of employees who can receive these each month, instead it is based on the contributions and achievements that have been made. Additionally, the group who is recognized in a particular year all come together for a celebratory luncheon at the end of the year.

"Hammering it Home Awards" - years of service recognition: North's years of service awards are called their Hammering it Home Awards, being a play on words based on their industry. Each anniversary, employees receive one of these awards and are sent an e-card. Beyond this, for significant milestones of five, 10, 15 years and beyond, they recognize employees with a plaque and a gift or gift card, ranging in value dependent upon the years of service. "We aim for the presentation of these awards to be done at an end of year party where we invite all staff and their partners, recognizing that such contributions are really significant and do at times have an impact on family too," says Cook.

TIPS

- **Seek out those who may not fully understand and/or embrace recognition.** For these individuals, make it personal to them by having a conversation about the difference recognition has made to them and the company, and how it's made them feel as they've either given or received recognition.

- **When introducing new people to the business, a thorough explanation of your recognition program should be a significant part of the onboarding process.** Those involved in the onboarding process should use the opportunity to reinforce the importance of your recognition programs, and explain how to use it from the onset.

Relay Payments

COMPANY

Relay Payments (Relay) is an end-to-end payment solution that takes the frustration out of lumper payments by providing instant, electronic payments in an industry historically reliant on cash and checks to conduct business. Founded in January 2019 by Ryan Droege and Spencer Barkoff, they're transforming their industry by focusing on building a customer experience unlike any other, while modernizing age-old payment processes in the supply chain industry.

Relay has around 110 employees in the U.S. and the Ukraine.

OVERVIEW

Relay is a fast-growing startup with a disruptive product roadmap and vision to help them meet their aggressive growth goals to transform the logistics industry. Key to this growth is their people strategy, which is being developed and led by Amy Zimmerman, Chief People Officer. "Relay has real potential to be the category winner, and I'm committed to helping them create the environment and infrastructure to drive that outcome," says Zimmerman.

Part of the people strategy involves the development of a comprehensive recognition program, a way to help fuel and drive this growth. "We had some basic recognition in place, but we decided that it was time to evolve it into something more comprehensive to not only reward and recognize, but to elevate people who inspire similar behaviors and the kind of innovation that will drive the business," says Zimmerman. The result is a multifaceted recognition program that recognizes and celebrates achievements exhibiting desired behaviors, and going above and beyond expectations to achieve milestones in their quest to transform an entire industry.

RECOGNITION PROGRAM

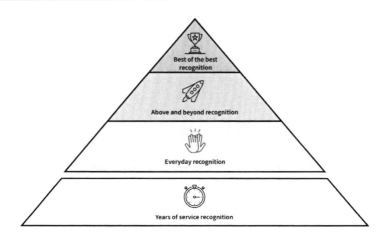

There are four levels and seven individual in Relay's recognition program:

 "Shout Outs" - anytime peer-to-peer social recognition: Everyday recognition is handled informally, with employees shouting out words of recognition through their online messaging tool.

 Anytime milestone pins: At Relay, employees receive a vest when they join the company and are awarded pins at certain milestones such as for product releases, when goals are hit or for anniversaries. Employees proudly wear and collect them, and they've become an integral part of their culture.

 "Relay Raves" - monthly peer-to-peer recognition: During the monthly "Relay Rally," which is what they call their monthly all-employee call, they have Relay Raves, which is when anyone calls out recognition to a colleague, celebrating these achievements together.

"Epic Effort Awards" - anytime manager awards: The next level is manager discretionary awards that can be given at any time based on persistent effort to meet urgent needs. Employees can receive a gift, paid time off or a meal for themselves and a guest.

 Quarterly manager-nominated values awards: To support and drive their values-led culture, the next level of recognition is Relay's quarterly values awards. Managers nominate employees for these, with Zimnmerman and the two founders selecting one winner for each of their three values. Each winner receives a pin, a $500 gift card and an exclusive and high-end swag gift.

 "Impact Awards" - annual peer-to-peer nominated awards: The next level is the Impact Awards, which are held annually, and where anyone can nominate a person who has made a huge impact on the business. The two winners are again selected by Zimmerman and the founders, with each winner receiving an all-inclusive paid trip for themselves and a guest.

 Years of service recognition: To recognize years of service, each anniversary year employees receive a new pin for their vest.

TIPS

- **Companies of all sizes should have recognition at their core.** No matter how new, small or fast-paced your business, it's important to make recognition an integral part of your business and people strategies.

- **Develop a multifaceted approach to recognition.** This can help drive and link your programs to innovation, higher performance, higher engagement and loyalty.

Reward Gateway

COMPANY

Reward Gateway is on a mission to "make the world a better place to work." They do this by helping more than 2,500 of the world's leading companies in 23 countries attract, engage and retain their people through an employee engagement platform that brings employee benefits, discounts and perks, recognition and reward, wellbeing, communications and surveys into one unified hub.

Reward Gateway has more than 500 employees located in Australia, Bulgaria, the U.K. and the U.S.

OVERVIEW

Recognition has always been a key element of Reward Gateway's EVP (employee value proposition), using it as a tool to help their workforce feel appreciated, aligning it with their mission, values and employer brand. Over the years, their recognition program has evolved as they've addressed the changing needs of their people and as they've worked towards creating a culture of recognition.

This evolution has happened in a variety of ways. From changing the name of the program from MORE! to Appreci8 to clearly state its purpose and reflect the eight values they recognize against, to changing the program design to make it more continuous and inclusive. They've also woven recognition into their communications strategy. "We've changed the language and focus of our communication, taking recognition principles and threading them through our other HR and internal communication practices, shining the light on and opening the door to recognition both directly and indirectly," says Catrin Lewis, Head of Global Engagement and Internal Communications.

Another example of evolving to meet the changing needs was a global virtual recognition event held on Employee Appreciation Day March 2021, at a time when many of their employees were still in lockdown because of COVID-19. They wanted to do something special, something incredible, to make each and every employee feel appreciated and to celebrate the contributions the teams had been making. The result was the "Thank You Festival," which had a theme of finding new ways to bring the Reward Gateway community together, doing so by including a lineup of four bands to appeal to a wide demographic, and having the leadership team share recognition messages across teams to show how connected they were even when working remotely.

The event was a huge success, with 87% of employees sending or receiving recognition e-cards on the day, with the same number of appreciation moments being shared in one day as to what is normally sent in a month. "We delivered an event that put a smile on our 500+ employees, and made a permanent mark in our wider community about how to make recognition a company-wide priority, with us smashing our initial goal for moments of recognition within the business and bringing people together across the world for a unique, shared experience accessible for all," says Lewis.

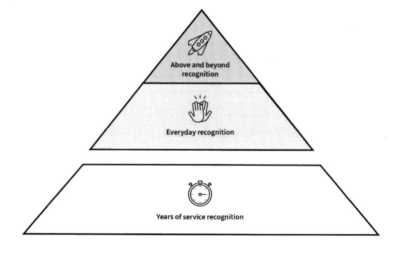

RECOGNITION PROGRAM

Above and beyond recognition

Everyday recognition

Years of service recognition

There are three levels and five individual plans in Reward Gateway's "Appreci8" recognition program:

 "High Fives" - anytime peer-to-peer e-cards: Reward Gateway has two kinds of e-cards that anyone can give at any time, and are shared on their digital social recognition wall. The first are their eight values e-cards, and the second are those that celebrate occasions, special activities and reaching business goals.

 Weekly CEO blog recognition: Every Monday, the CEO of Reward Gateway shares a blog on their engagement platform for everyone to see. It's their most popular piece of content and it's used as a place to shout out to those contributing to the mission, goals and really pushing the needle. The visibility and recognition from their leader makes this moment one of the employees' favorites, and can be a great boost to focus and motivate the individuals or teams highlighted.

 "You Rock Awards" - anytime peer-to-peer awards: The next level are their You Rock Awards, which are point-based awards that anyone can give to their colleagues at any time for awesome work demonstrating their values. Each employee can give 12 a year. Points can be used to select items through the Reward Marketplace, for company swag, or a variety of other things such as lunch with the CEO or special experiences for employees. "We've broadened our offering over the years to make it personalized to the individual," says Lewis.

 "Game Changer Awards" - anytime manager awards: The top level are Game Changer Awards, which managers can give to anyone at any time for going above and beyond in demonstrating their values. Recipients are again awarded points, which can be used in the same way as the previous level of awards. Budgets are set as a guideline for managers, and more can be requested if they are all given out.

Years of service recognition: Service is recognized at Reward Gateway every year in a non-financial way. This is done by sending special anniversary e-cards and also having a shout out through the weekly "People News" section on "boom!," their communications platform.

TIPS

- **Integrate recognition into your various ways of working.** Keep in mind that recognition on its own is not as powerful as when you integrate it into your other ways of working, giving it a super boost through your communications and other company actions and activities.

- **Use recognition as a way to foster and nurture a community, using it as a way to help connect your workforce and build strong relationships.** Keep this in mind as you design your recognition programs, not focusing everything on the individual, bringing community into your recognition design and practices.

Roche Pharmaceuticals

COMPANY

Roche Pharmaceuticals (Roche), one of the world's leading research-based healthcare companies, has been committed to improving lives since the company was founded in 1896 in Basel, Switzerland. Today, Roche creates innovative medicines and diagnostic tests that help millions of patients globally.

Roche has over 90,000 employees located in more than 100 countries who work across their three business areas.

OVERVIEW

At Roche, they believe that personalized approaches achieve the best outcomes for their patients. The same is true with their employees, as they take an individual approach to create opportunities that enable them to bring their unique selves to Roche and achieve their best work on behalf of their patients.

The same goes with their approach to recognition, with personalization built into their global and local recognition programs so that everyone at Roche, no matter what they do or where they work, feels valued in a meaningful and memorable way. This is done by using a variety of formats and options throughout the program to respect cultural and personal differences, letting employees decide when and how to recognize one another.

"Throughout our recognition programs we try to reinforce the simplicity of the thank you, how one recognition moment can make a difference in how you feel," says Nebel Crowhurst, People & Culture Director - U.K.

To end, let me say that Roche has a dedicated squad who is currently reviewing their recognition programs in light of changes being made to their evolving performance management practice. "As we move away from traditional annual appraises to more frequent ones, we want to reimagine and connect this to our Applause program," says Crowhurst.

RECOGNITION PROGRAM

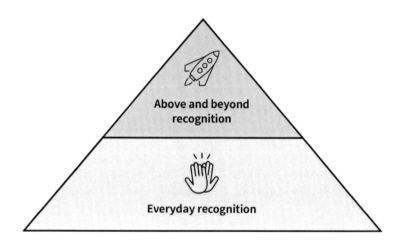

There are two levels and three individual plans in Roche's U.K. "Applause" recognition program:

 Anytime peer-to-peer eCards: Roche created e-cards ranging from a simple thank you, to ones related to their three values, to those that encourage or highlight certain desired behaviors. Employees can choose the e-card that is right for the situation and the colleague, and can even create their own personalized e-card to create a more meaningful recognition moment.

An example of an e-card to recognize and reinforce behaviors related to a key business strategy are their "One Roche" e-cards. These encourage the move from working independently to crossing over and sharing between the three business areas, doing so with a "One Roche" mindset

The e-cards are primarily encouraged to be used as a mechanism for appreciation, and while there is no monetary value attached to them, the purpose is to encourage a culture in which people feel valued and inclined to offer open thanks and appreciation to one another.

 Anytime peer-to-peer awards: The next level is peer-to-peer awards that recognize colleagues for work above and beyond normal role expectations, stepping up without necessarily being asked to do so. Employees receive a small number of points to spend instantly, without manager approval, on their reward platform. This again has a level of personalization, as there are no strict guidelines on how many points should be awarded for each situation, just a range provided for guidance.

 Anytime manager approved peer-to-peer awards: The next level is awards that give a larger number of reward points to be spent on their reward platform, and require manager approval. This signoff is less about approvals, and more about ensuring a consistent and fair approach.

There are three levels to these awards, with guidance provided to allow discretion and personalization as well as fairness and consistency. Here are examples from the criteria provided to employees:

1. Recognition for a remarkable accomplishment with an impeccable mindset and level of effort.

2. Recognition for an extraordinary piece of work with exceptional outcomes or behavior.

3. Recognition for phenomenal work which showed unique thinking, required leadership or risk-taking with a positive company impact.

TIPS:

- **Build personalization into your recognition programs.** Let employees decide what and how they want to recognize one another to make the biggest impact.

- **Add an element of flexibility and adaptation to your recognition programs.**
  At Roche, leaders are empowered to make local ad hoc decisions on further recognition, providing personalized opportunities to show appreciation. From taking teams out to eat together, to offering additional annual leave, bring uniqueness to the experience of appreciation in ways that mean the most to people.

Shell Energy Retail

COMPANY

Shell Energy Retail supplies 100% renewable electricity, as well as gas, smart home technology, broadband and exclusive rewards to homes in Britain. They aim to make it easy for customers to choose the best home energy options for them, and guide them to a better, cleaner, energy future.

Shell Energy Retail has over 1,800 employees based across the U.K., Poland and Germany.

OVERVIEW

When Shell Energy Retail launched its company values in July 2020, the team decided to use recognition as a way to help celebrate and embed them across the business, and at the same time, move to a consistent global approach. They brought together an internal group of employees called BIG (Business Involvement Group) to help with this, sharing ideas, contributing different views and perspectives and gaining local buy-in.

The result is "Shine," which is the name selected by the members of BIG for the recognition program, aligning with who they are as an energy business. The program was launched in November 2020, and as Thomas Dibble, HR Project Manager says, "It was designed to drive a culture where everyone says thank you to everyone by focusing on peer-to-peer recognition." Figures jumped from around 40 colleagues sharing circa 300 e-cards pre-launch to over 150 colleagues sharing over 2,400 pieces of recognition in November 2020, with the number rising the following month and more than 100 colleagues consistently sharing recognition since launch.

RECOGNITION PROGRAM

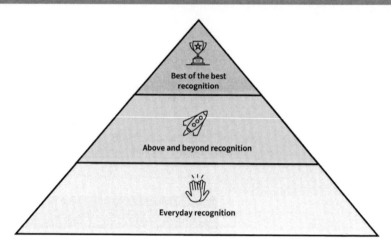

There are three levels and four individual plans in Shell Energy Retail's "Shine" recognition program:

 Anytime peer-to-peer e-cards: They created e-cards that employees can send to one another at any time through their recognition platform with the intention to be a quick and easy way to display a message of thanks, congratulations, well done and so on.

 Anytime manager gifts: All managers are given a budget which they can spend on ad hoc personalized gifts for their team members. They are given the discretion to decide when and what to give based on what the individual or team has done, what the individual likes, and the overall impact and message they'd like the gift to convey.

 "Shine Awards" - monthly peer-to-peer nominated awards: To bring the values to life, and further encourage peer-to-peer recognition, the main features of Shine are the nominations which lead to monthly awards. Employees can nominate one another for demonstrating behaviors associated with their values, and for those that truly live and breathe them. A rotating panel of managers from different teams reviews the monthly nominations and selects the winners, with the top three receiving £50 (or local equivalent)

into their recognition account, and the next two receiving £30 (or local equivalent) into their account.

 "Shine Awards" - quarterly peer-to-peer nominated awards: The top three winners of the monthly awards are automatically entered into the quarterly awards, which are voted on by their Executive Team. All employees receive a personalized e-card from the member of the Executive Team who reviewed the nominations, regardless of whether or not they were selected as one of the best nominations of the quarter. The Executive Team will choose the top two nominations per value of the quarter, who are then invited to a VIP annual awards event, where there will be a "Values Champion" crowned for each of the values – showcasing which employee has been the best embodiment of one of the company's core values.

In addition, anyone who receives three or more nominations for the same value gets a digital badge for that value which they can display in their email signature. "Since we have offices in multiple different locations, we wanted something which could be displayed to all colleagues regardless of where they were, in a similar way to having physical badges on a lanyard, showcasing colleagues living our values. It also gives recipients the opportunity to continually display how they've been a true champion to our values," says Dibble.

Celebrating our people

TIPS

- **Understand and address global differences in your recognition program.** At Shell Energy they have done this by adapting their recognition program for colleagues in Germany due to local employment and GDPR laws, creating a slightly different nomination process. They felt it was better to adapt it than to exclude them from their global program, thus ensuring that all employees across the business can be recognized, and recognise one another, for their contributions.

- **Find ways to showcase recognition in your own unique way.** At Shell Energy they do this with their virtual badges, which act as a way to showcase recognition achievements each and every time an email is sent from one employee to another.

Southern New Hampshire University

COMPANY

Southern New Hampshire University (SNHU) is a private, nonprofit, accredited institution with more than 3,000 on-campus students and over 150,000 online students. Since its founding in 1932, the University has transformed from a school of accounting and secretarial science into an institution offering over 200 programs, with a mission to transform the lives of learners.

SNHU has 10,000+ employees working in their various locations across the U.S.

OVERVIEW

At SNHU they are not only focused on transforming the lives of their students, but of their employees, doing so through a strategic objective to attract, develop, empower and retain world-class talent. This has created a strong culture, one that for the last 14 years has made the honor roll for the "Great Colleges to Work For" survey.

A key part of SNHU's culture is listening to their people, doing so through monthly surveys. Through the surveys, they identified the need and opportunity to change their approach to recognition, something that time and time again came out top on their employees' list of what mattered most to them.

The team conducted an audit to understand the current state of their recognition programs.They found that there were 200 different ones, with 26% of them tied to performance, focusing on what was being produced and not who was doing it and how they were being done. They also held additional employee focus groups to gather feedback, better understand their recognition needs and get input on the recognition systems that worked best for them.

"We set ourselves the objective of transforming the lives of our people through recognition, creating an approach and culture to deliver recognition in a meaningful way and create a sense of connection and belonging," says Jennifer LaFountain, Director of Talent Engagement & Inclusion.

Next, the recognition proposal was presented to the leadership team for approval, using a creative multimedia approach that included showcasing the technology and playing extracts from employee focus group sessions. "We wanted to show our leaders what recognition could look like so that they wouldn't be able to say no," says LaFountain.

Once approved, they designed their program based on two key objectives:

1. **Flexible** - Flexibility is key in the design of their program to reflect the diverse needs of their people. One example is with the inclusion of four appreciation languages, or what SNHU calls "appreciation preferences" (e.g. tangible gifts, words of affirmation, quality time and acts of service). These help employees identify what is important to them so that others can recognize them in the most meaningful way.

2. **Phased** - SNHU opted for a phased approach to the launch of their recognition program, not putting all elements of recognition in from the start. They began with non-financial recognition, doing so to "change the hearts and minds of our people," says LaFountain. Moving forward they will review and consider financial recognition, again putting something in place that is flexible and aligns with the culture and values of their organization.

"We are at the start of our recognition journey. During this first phase we have built a recognition foundation to acknowledge the great work our people are doing and put it under the spotlight. Much of what we're doing is building the recognition muscle, getting employees to recognize one another as well as understand the value of not just saying thank you, but strategically linking it to our values," says LaFountain.

RECOGNITION PROGRAM

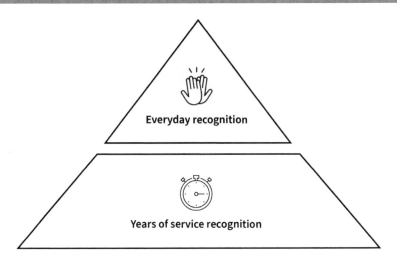

There are two levels and two individual plans in SNHU's "Shine" recognition program:

 Anytime peer-to-peer e-cards: SNHU has three kinds of e-cards that they are trialing and testing during the first phase of their recognition program launch. The first are values-based e-cards that recognize employees for actions and behaviors aligned with their five company values. Next, are their greetings e-cards that recognize and celebrate occasions and activities, including welcome to the team, happy birthday, and get well soon. These e-Cards were designed by employees, thus getting them involved and engaged with them. And finally, they have e-cards to recognize the four appreciation languages mentioned earlier.

Years of service recognition: SNHU has started to change their approach to years of service during this first phase of their recognition journey. In the past, they only recognized employees after five years, which meant that only 32% of employees were eligible, and 52% of employees left before hitting this milestone.

Because of this, and to align with their strategy and employees' needs, they introduced non-financial recognition at every year of service. Now, their recognition system automatically does three things: It sends an anniversary e-card to the employee, it notifies the manager so they can recognize their employee and it posts the announcement on their social recognition wall so that others can celebrate the milestone. During the next phase, they will review and develop a consistent approach to financial recognition at key milestones.

TIPS

- **Involve your employees in the development and ongoing running of your recognition program.** At SNHU they did this by creating an engagement squad to help design and deliver the program, and having champions to keep momentum and spark interest going forward. They even use this team to develop training videos to inspire and motivate others to give meaningful recognition.

- **Consider a phased approach to recognition.** A phased approach can help you begin to build the core foundation of your recognition culture. At SNHU they've done this by having phase one focus on non-financial recognition before moving to other phases that will introduce financial recognition, but it's up to you to decide what will work best based on your culture and objectives.

Teleperformance

COMPANY

Teleperformance is a global leader in providing exceptional omnichannel customer experience, connecting customers with the world's most successful companies.

Teleperformance has 380,000 employees, working in 450 sites across 83 countries. In the U.K. and South Africa, they have just over 12,000 employees.

OVERVIEW

When Teleperformance's U.K./South Africa CEO joined the business in April 2019, they had a global "Circle of Excellence" recognition program, which recognized the top 1%, but not the remaining 99% of employees. So with feedback gained from employees from across the company, they set out to develop a program that met these five objectives:

1. Was inclusive of all employees regardless of role, level or department.

2. Recognized their high flyers and top performers.

3. Recognized those going above and beyond based on their five company values.

4. Recognized those going above and beyond for their teammates, customers, clients and communities.

5. Celebrated the "moments that matter" to simply say thank you and celebrate milestones and special moments.

Their new program was launched in January 2020, and has not only achieved these objectives, but has received accolades from their workforce as well as industry awards.

RECOGNITION PROGRAM

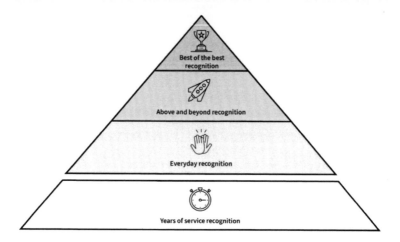

There are four levels and six individual plans in Teleperformance U.K./South Africa's recognition program:

 Anytime peer-to-peer e-cards: Teleperformance has a full suite of e-cards that employees can send to one another to cover the "moments that matter," including birthdays, anniversaries, religious holidays and events from their annual awareness calendar.

 "Shout Outs" - anytime peer-to-peer recognition: In addition, they have a dedicated Shout Out online channel that supports spreading gratitude, thanks and praise between colleagues. "We want recognition and gratitude to be second nature as a way to say thank you and to celebrate successes. We've tried to encompass moments that matter to cover performance, values, humanity and just uplifting spirits," says Lisa Dolan, SVP of Employee Engagement and Global Head of Diversity, Equity and Inclusion.

They've done this by also holding campaigns throughout the year. An example was for National Espresso Day, where special e-cards were sent with tag lines such as "Thanks a Latte" and "Sip Sip Hooray," along with coffee vouchers given out by leaders.

THANKS A
LATTE

Thank you for all your hard
work and commitment to
Teleperformance

 "Superstar Awards" - monthly peer-to-peer nominated awards: The next level recognizes colleagues for going above and beyond for teammates, customers, clients and the local community. These celebrate the wonderful things people are doing from a humanity perspective. Each month over 600 nominations are received, with around 100-150 being selected as the overall winners. The CEO then announces the winners in a virtual awards ceremony, and they receive a pin badge, certificate and £25 worth of points loaded into their benefits account.

 "Culture Awards" - monthly peer-to-peer nominated awards: Next are the monthly Culture Awards, which are more prestigious as they recognize colleagues for living and breathing the company values. It follows the same peer-to-peer nomination process, and receives around 300 nominations each month, with around 50 employees being selected as winners. Winners are announced at the virtual award ceremony, and receive a badge pin for the specific value, a certificate and £25 worth of points.

"Circle of Excellence Awards" - annual awards: The final level is a global program, which recognizes the top 1% from across the organization annually. It is based on a scorecard/stack ranking matrix, showing how employees perform against a set of KPI's and metrics. Winners receive a badge pin, a certificate and £50 worth of points.

 Years of service recognition: Long service is recognized in a variety of ways at Teleperformance U.K., with badge pins, certificates and points being awarded similar to other recognition programs starting at three years of service. In addition, starting at one year of service, employees receive additional days of leave to be taken during the anniversary year, and for years five, 10 and 20, additional weeks or months of paid leave. "Paid leave is offered as this is what our employees said they wanted at the time when the scheme was being designed. They didn't want gifts from a catalog but extra time to spend with their family and friends, this is why we introduced Gift Days," says Dolan.

TIPS

- **Develop a program that addresses your entire workforce.** Put something in place that everyone can be a part of, celebrating and recognizing all moments that matter.

- **Keep your program simple.** Recognition doesn't have to be complex and doesn't have to cost a lot. Saying thank you and giving praise is something everyone can do at any time, and makes a huge difference to the way the recipient feels and the pleasure it gives by making someone smile.

University of Lincoln

COMPANY

The University of Lincoln is a fast-growing, gold-rated university that is one of the largest employers in the city of Lincoln, U.K. They are proud to be home to world-class researchers who are making profound contributions to their subject areas. From developing new medical technologies to preserving architectural treasures, Lincoln's academic community is changing the world.

The University of Lincoln has more than 1,800 employees located in the U.K.

OVERVIEW

At the University of Lincoln, half of their employees are academics, a group that generally receives recognition externally through publishing papers and speaking at conferences. But the other half received no recognition, and in addition, there was nothing in place to connect the two halves in order to drive collaboration and recognition across the entire University.

These are the challenges that the University faced as they developed their recognition strategy and programs. The result was programs that focus on the recognition and less on the awards, using it as an opportunity to thank one another, celebrate successes, and, being in the education sector, help one another learn and grow. "We intentionally give moderate awards as we believe that the recognition is more important than the money," says Ian Hodson, Head of Reward.

In addition to the formal program, from time-to-time the University gives recognition awards to all employees to thank and recognize them for their contributions. For example, an award was given in July 2021 at the end of the academic year as a way to thank employees for getting through a tough year due to the challenges of COVID-19. Everyone was given £50 which was loaded into their recognition account, which employees could spend on themselves or pool together to buy something to share.

Another example is an award given for achieving their strategic objectives, which again was in the amount of £50. "We wanted something to align everyone with our objectives, pulling in the same direction, and to thank them for when we achieved them," says Hodson.

RECOGNITION PROGRAM

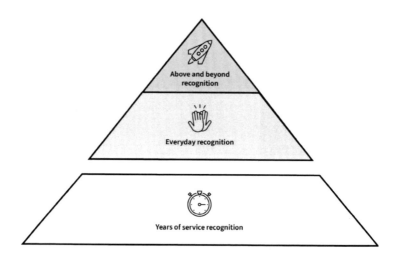

There are three levels and three individual plans in the University of Lincoln's recognition program:

 Anytime peer-to-peer e-cards: They have three types of e-cards that employees can send to one another at any time through their recognition platform. The first are ones that align with their values. The second are those that connect employees and celebrate events such as birthdays. And the third are ones that allow colleagues to check in with each other and open dialogue in a social way to support more flexible ways of working where the social aspects of the workplace can be harder to create. Copies of all e-cards go to managers so that they can engage with and follow-up directly with their employees.

 Annual peer-to-peer nominated awards: The other element is their annual awards, which employees can nominate one another for based on the following categories:

- Individual awards given for demonstrating their values.

- Team achievement awards given for working together to achieve strategic objectives.

- Development awards given for completing accredited development programs.

- Teaching excellence awards which are put forward by students.

- Research awards given for excellence in research.

Winners are selected by a panel, and are invited to attend an event to celebrate their achievements and where the vice chancellor presents them with a certificate. "We attempt to mirror with our staff what we do with our students when we present them with their graduation certificate, symbolizing their achievements and contributions. You can see how much it means to them as they carefully handle the certificate, and how their five seconds of fame means the world to them," says Hodson.

The award amounts range from £100 to £300 for individual awards, which are loaded into their recognition account. For team awards, they're given £500 to be used for team development activities.

 Years of service recognition: Starting at six months, employees receive an e-card to recognize and celebrate their time with the University. This is generated through the system and sent annually, with managers again being notified so they don't miss these important milestones.

TIPS

- **Think about the best people to select the winners of your awards.** At the University, they wanted their managers to engage with and trust their annual awards, so for all awards with the exception of team ones, they gave managers the discretion to select winners. The HR team moderates them to ensure fairness, equity and consistency, but ultimately managers are the decision-makers.

- **Find ways to share and showcase recognition awards and stories.** At the University, they take case studies from their annual awards and weave them into their induction process to show what good looks like and to highlight how recognition is done.

Watford Community Housing

COMPANY

Watford Community Housing (WCH) own and manage more than 5,000 homes across South-West Hertfordshire, U.K., with a focus on providing much-needed homes for lower-income households. Their aim is to make a real difference by delivering better homes and supporting their communities.

WCH has 175 employees, of which 40% work offsite supporting their customers.

OVERVIEW

WCH had an old-fashioned approach to recognition, having programs that did not sit or link together, and ones that were not tied to a strategy. They set out to review this along with their other reward elements such as base and variable pay, and their overall benefits package. The result are programs that are firmly based on transparency and fairness, designing and delivering them in genuine and meaningful ways. This has served them well, with employee satisfaction increasing from 53% to 81% in just two years.

From a recognition perspective, WCH describes it as a "smorgasbord approach." Employees range from plumbers and electricians to accountants, construction managers and customer service professionals, so a "one-size-fits-all" approach would not meet everyone's needs. Instead, they created different ways to give and receive recognition, giving employees a choice for what works for them, with a focus on encouraging people to say thank you and to make others feel appreciated.

RECOGNITION PROGRAM

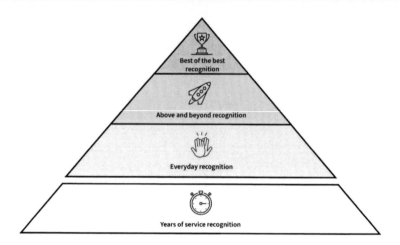

There are four levels and five individual plans in WCH's recognition program:

 Anytime peer-to-peer postcards and e-cards: WCH began with physical recognition postcards that were linked to their three values, and could be sent to one another at any time. It was a very physical process, with postcards being written and put into post boxes, and then a member of the HR team once a week collecting, recording and handing them out. Their employees loved them, so they decided to layer onto these digital e-cards that look the same, but can be sent quicker and more easily to colleagues both in and outside of the office. By having both, it gives their diverse workforce the choice to use whichever works best for them.

 Anytime director awards: At the next level, all directors can give an award of up to £50 at any time to reward members of their team for going above and beyond. There is a rough budget for these awards, but it can be modified should it be necessary.

 Quarterly peer-to-peer nominated awards: Next, each quarter employees can nominate one another for living up to and exceeding their values. The executive team selects the three winners, who receive £25, and are also automatically rolled into the annual award process.

 Annual peer-to-peer nominated awards: And finally, at the end of the year all quarterly award winners are eligible to receive an annual award. In addition to the three values awards, there are also awards for the team of the year, manager of the year, and the Colin Heinisch award, which commemorates a much-loved employee who passed away, and is for the employee with the most positive attitude.

The winners are voted on by employees, giving them the chance to own and feel like a part of the process, making it egalitarian and transparent. Winners receive their awards during an annual recognition event, being given a trophy, flowers and £75.

 Years of service recognition: Service awards are given at five, 10, 15 and 20 years of service. For five years, they receive an extra day of leave to be taken that year, and for the other years they are invited onto stage during the annual recognition event to receive flowers and a special gift that has been selected just for them.

TIPS

- **Be transparent in how you run and communicate your recognition program**. For example, at WCH they removed long service awards, not explaining why, and no surprise, employees were not happy with this. They recently re-introduced them, doing them in a different way to align with their new recognition strategy, explaining this to their employees in a transparent way.

- **Understand your workforce.** For example, At WCH they have employees who still prefer postcards over e-cards. Had they removed them, it would have disengaged this part of their workforce, with them missing out on this important program.

Youi

Youi, which stands for You Insure, is an Australian company providing insurance for cars and vehicles, home and contents, and businesses. Their mission is to be Australia's most trusted insurance company, challenging existing practices and giving people a better insurance alternative.

Youi has 1,440 employees located across Australia.

OVERVIEW

Youi's recognition program began as a way to recognize high performance to drive and support their growth ambitions as a startup. But when the theme of recognition came up time and time again in employee surveys, they knew that as the company grew and matured they needed to revisit it, challenging existing practices in the same way they do with their business and products. As Ryan McGrory, Head of Employee Experience & Communications, says, "We wanted to do something really big, making our recognition program more inclusive and more aligned with our culture and our new ways of working. We were so serious about it that we added 'Recognition' as our sixth company value."

They embarked on a discovery project, meeting with leaders and employees at different levels and from different functions, asking the question - what does it take to be a great Youi citizen? This resulted in a huge list of milestones and actions such as joining the company, attending development sessions, providing feedback to others, volunteering, and supporting customers or colleagues, which were used to develop their comprehensive new recognition program. "We wanted to capture and then recognize all of the elements, dimensions and contributions made by our people throughout their employee experience," says McGrory.

Youi's new recognition program is called "YourGame," reflecting the gamification approach and mechanics incorporated into the design. By adopting these in a non-game context, they've been able to not only drive recognition, but also behavioral changes found by gamification researchers such as helping to improve engagement levels, assist in completing certain tasks, and encourage and improve personal learning and development. They've seen fantastic relationships between YourGame usage and participation in these activities - for example in the first six months they saw a 47% increase in completing e-learning assessments and 35% increase in participating in wellbeing activities. And more recently, when measuring the impact on customer service, they've seen almost double the average number of "Awesome" customer service reviews than in the previous two years.

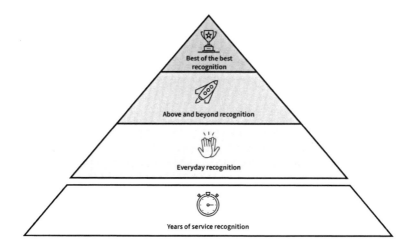

RECOGNITION PROGRAM

Best of the best recognition

Above and beyond recognition

Everyday recognition

Years of service recognition

There are four levels and four individual plans in Youi's "Your Game" recognition program:

 Anytime peer-to-peer points and e-cards: The cornerstone of YourGame are the points that are awarded and the e-cards sent through the platform for actions and behaviors exhibited that reflect those mapped out and loaded into the system. Some are awarded automatically, e.g. joining the company, attending a class, sending feedback, while others are awarded by colleagues in recognition of contributions aligned with their company values. The points awarded are based on their internal value system, e.g. those requiring more effort and impact receive more points.

Every month there are multiple draws which all employees with points are entered into, and where they can win a variety of prizes. "We do this to create a fun and positive experience for our people. They love the inclusive feeling of being involved and it's crazy the things people do to win prizes such as a branded t-shirt," says McGrory.

 Monthly peer-to-peer nominated awards: The next level are monthly awards that each department runs separately, which are based on two things - achieving department KPI's and demonstrating company values. Employees can nominate one another for these awards, with the leadership team selecting the winners who get recognized publicly, receive a cash award, and are invited to a quarterly winner's lunch that is hosted by an executive.

 Biannual peer-to-peer nominated awards: The top level awards align with the timing of their biannual company meetings, using them as an opportunity to celebrate those who make greater and/or longer-term impacts on customers, colleagues and the business. These awards are again based on achieving KPIs and demonstrating values, with employees nominating one another, and leaders selecting winners. The winners receive a voucher, VIP dinner event with the executive team, certificate, profile in company-wide newsletter, and they unlock a badge in the Game.

Years of service recognition: Each service anniversary is celebrated at Youi, with points and an e-card being sent automatically, as well as a branded t-shirt specifically designed for that year. In addition, for every three years of service employees receive a cash bonus, and after 10 years they receive a three-month paid leave (which is standard in Australia) as well as an invitation to a VIP event and a special badge in the Game.

TIPS

- **Align your recognition program and tactics with your culture.** Critically evaluate your recognition program to make sure it fits your culture as it changes and evolves.

- **Look at everyday moments when you map out what you'll recognize.** Look at the end-to-end employee experience, including what happens every day, to determine exactly what you want to recognize. At Youi they did this through their intense mapping exercise, looking end-to-end at the employee experience to capture all of those important recognition opportunities and moments.

Zappos

COMPANY

Zappos, which is an adaptation of "zapatos," the Spanish word for shoes, began in 1999 as a small, online retailer that only sold shoes. Today, they still sell shoes as well as clothing, handbags, accessories and more. That "more" is providing the very best customer service, customer experience and company culture. They aim to inspire the world by showing it's possible to simultaneously deliver happiness to customers, employees, vendors, shareholders and the community in a long-term, sustainable way.

Zappos has around 1,500 employees located in the U.S. and Canada.

OVERVIEW

At Zappos, they believe that anything worth doing is worth doing with WOW, which they define as "doing something a little unconventional and innovative that has an emotional impact on the receiver." And when it comes to recognition, they've absolutely delivered wow in both the depth and breadth of their formal and informal recognition programs, going above and beyond to help their employees, or what they call "Zapponians," feel appreciated.

Recognition at Zappos started out very basic, with the HR team hand-decorating stars that were put on sticks to look like magic wands, and presenting them to employees to proudly display at their desks. Since then, a variety of new recognition plans have been added that let employees decide how best to wow one another. "We don't believe in a one-size-fits-all approach, we want to provide different ways to recognize so that our people can pick and choose what speaks to them and their team culture," said Maritza Lewis, Employee Engagement Manager.

Another way they've delivered wow is by evolving the individual plans. One example is their "Zappos Zollars Awards," which began as paper money that leaders could give out to be redeemed for one of five gifts. It's now digital money that anyone can give out, and can be redeemed for gift cards, swag gifts or even as a donation to charity.

And yet another way is with their approach to years of service awards, which again is not only innovative but delivers wow in a meaningful way. After speaking with a social psychologist, who explained that having something visual would create a deeper connection and feeling of appreciation, they decided to have personalized license plates designed to symbolize years of service recognition. These are given out from year one, with colors changing every five years, and are proudly displayed for all to see and celebrate.

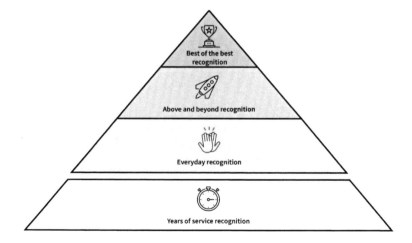

RECOGNITION PROGRAM

Best of the best recognition

Above and beyond recognition

Everyday recognition

Years of service recognition

There are four levels and five individual plans in Zappos's recognition program:

 Anytime informal discretionary recognition: The first level of recognition at Zappos is discretionary, with each team adopting their own method and approach. For example, the HR team does something they call "snaps," which is when they shout out recognition messages to one another during their weekly calls, snapping as this is done to celebrate these achievements together.

 "Zappos Zollars" - anytime peer-to-peer awards: The next level is Zappos Zollars, which is what they call their internal currency, and can be awarded by anyone through their digital platform at any time to fellow Zapponians for living their company values. Once signed off by HR, the recipient can choose from a variety of gifts – from a gift card, to company swag, to donating to charity, to bath bombs or food. The award offering is constantly being refreshed, with frequent check-ins with employees to find out what is right for them.

 "Co-Worker Bonus" - anytime peer-to-peer cash awards: The next level was introduced as an experiment, but has become so popular that it's now a key element of their recognition program. As with Zappos Zollars, a bonus can be awarded by anyone through their digital platform at any time to fellow Zapponians for living their company values. Each month, employees have $50 they can award as cash rewards, either all to one colleague or as two $25 awards. These awards are not carried over from month to month, and do require signoff by HR.

 "GOAT Award" - monthly leadership award: The top level is their GOAT Award, which stands for greatest of all time, and is an award that has been developed for the customer loyalty team. Leaders from this group each month nominate someone who has really gone above and beyond, and then together select the person who most deserves the award. The recipient receives a life-size toy goat, a $250 gift card and is recognized in a company-wide email to share their story and celebrate their achievements.

 Years of service recognition: Employees are recognized every year at Zappos. In their first year they receive a personalized license plate along with some Zappos Zollars. In subsequent years they receive a sticker similar to what you get from the DMV (Department of Motor Vehicles) to show that your car is registered for another year and an increased amount of Zappos Zollars. The color of the license plates change every five years to show these important milestones.

TIPS

- **Be experimental, trying out different approaches to recognition.** At Zappos they are constantly doing this, each time letting their employees know that it's an experiment, and may or may not be continued so as to set expectations.

- **Look for ways to create visual recognition moments**. Use visuals as a way to create a deeper connection and feeling of appreciation.

Zoom

Zoom is a global company that helps businesses and individuals bring teams, family and friends together in an easy, reliable and frictionless cloud platform. Committed to delivering happiness, believing that the greatest, most sustainable happiness comes from making others happy, they deliver this through their platform every single day.

Zoom has 5,000 employees located around the world.

OVERVIEW

With a company that is committed to delivering happiness, it should come as no surprise that recognition is at the core of who they are. Underpinned by their values that center around the concept of "We Care," this translates into how they design and deliver recognition for their employees, or what they call "Zoomies."

The goal of the program is as Lynne Oldham, Chief People Officer, says, "To make sure that when people do something extraordinary, or not so extraordinary, they feel recognized by the company, their manager, and their teammates."

What makes their program unique is that it is not owned by Human Resources, but by their Happy Crew, which is a volunteer team of 200 employees from around the world. Over the years they've added to the program, creating one that recognizes individuals and teams in different ways and at different times.

Another unique aspect of the program is that one part, the Executive Quarterly Awards, is not just for the employee, but for their family, all being treated to a meal. "We believe it takes a village, and that our families are very much involved in who we are at work, and so we want the family to also partake in the award," says Oldham.

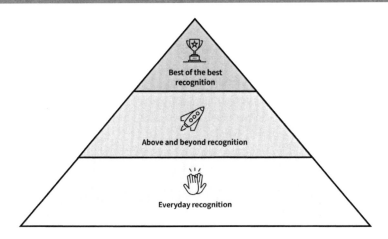

There are three levels and four individual plans in Zoom's recognition program:

 Anytime peer-to-peer social recognition: Recognition happens organically and regularly within Zoom's chat function, with employees writing notes of thanks at any time for others to see and comment on.

In addition, they do what Oldham calls "pile ons," which is when a senior leader shares the positive words received from a customer, with others piling on, jumping in and celebrating the great job the employee has done.

 Anytime peer-to-peer awards: These awards are the start of Zoom's formal recognition program, and are to recognize when someone has gone above and beyond or has helped out a colleague. Anyone at any time can nominate someone for an award, with the Happy Crew signing off, and the employee receiving a recognition note along with the opportunity to select a gift from a catalogue ranging from a value of $25-50 or donate the amount to charity. The awards have recently moved to recognize based on "Zoom abilities," their company values, acting to embed these into their language and actions.

 "Zoomie of the Quarter" - quarterly peer-to-peer nominated awards: For the next level, employees can nominate one another for quarterly awards, with all employees voting on the winners. These again are based on Zoom abilities, and winners, runners up and second runner ups receive financial awards ranging from $350 for winners and $150 for runner ups. Again, they can select gifts or donate the money to charity.

To add to the impact of this award, they are announced by the CEO during the all hands calls, reading out the name along with a snippet from the nomination. "We don't care if it takes five or 15 minutes, we want to verbally recognize our people," says Oldham.

 Quarterly executive nominated awards: Another element of the quarterly awards are ones that are run by the executive team. Members of the executive team come together each quarter to nominate individuals and teams outside of their own group based on going above and beyond against their Zoom abilities.

Winners receive a meal for themselves and their families, for as mentioned previously, Zoom believes that the family should be a part of the recognition as they have contributed to the achievements. And, like the other quarterly awards, winners are announced during the all hands calls.

TIPS

- **Consider the ownership of your program.** For instance, think about how your program can be owned, co-owed, supported, etc. by others outside of Human Resources to increase its effectiveness and usage.

- **Find ways for recognition to support and drive collaboration across your business.** At Zoom, this is seen in the Executive Quarterly Awards, with nominations intentionally coming from outside of the executive's responsibility areas to drive awareness, understanding and appreciation of what individuals and teams are doing across the business.

Conclusion

Let me end the way I began, with a call to action and a call to change. I encourage you to challenge yourself and your organization to take a step back and evaluate why, what, when and how you show appreciation through recognition, and build or rebuild your recognition pyramid and informal recognition practices to be ones that truly meet the changing needs of your people and your business. By doing this, I believe that together we can create a world where every person genuinely feels appreciated and where recognition freely and naturally flows.

I could end here, with this upbeat and hopefully inspirational thought, but I'm too practical to do this. So let me next say that I know from personal experience that the change I'm encouraging you to take can be difficult and that sometimes you will get pushback from your business leaders, trying to stop you from doing what you know is right. I had this at a previous company when my CEO thought that recognition was paying our sales team a commission, and it was a long and painful road to get him to understand that this was not the case. But don't give up, remember all of the benefits of appreciation that were shared at the start, and take one small step at a time to overcome obstacles and drive the change you know your business needs.

And since change may be daunting to you, my final gift is to share some tips on change and rethinking from Adam Grant's book *Think Again*. It's a fantastic book that challenges us to reevaluate our opinions and decisions, moving from the "comfort of convictions to the discomfort of doubt." In it, he shares 30 takeaways for rethinking, of which I've shared three to start you on your path to change.

1. **Think like a scientist**. When you start forming an opinion, resist the temptation to preach, prosecute or politick. Treat your emerging view as a hunch or a hypothesis and test it with data.

2. **Define your identity in terms of values, not opinions**. It's easier to avoid getting stuck to your past beliefs if you don't become attached to them as part of your present self-

concept. See yourself as someone who values curiosity, learning, mental flexibility and searching for knowledge.

3. **Seek out information that goes against your views**. You can fight confirmation bias, burst filter bubbles and escape echo chambers by actively engaging with ideas that challenge your assumptions. An easy place to start is to follow people who make you think – even if you usually disagree with what they think.

So that's it from me, let me wish you all the best on your appreciation and recognition journey. I'd love to see and hear what you do next, so do share them with me and with others, paying it forward by inspiring and supporting one another. I know we'd all *Appreciate It!*

Acknowledgements

This book has been a true collaborative effort, and for that I am most grateful. Whether you helped me directly by agreeing to be interviewed, or indirectly by inspiring me through the books you wrote, let me thank you for helping me create a rich and diverse collection of thoughts, tips and stories. I learned so much writing the book, and I'm confident that all those that read it will as well.

Let me start out by thanking my "playwrights," those of you who were kind enough to let me interview you and share your wonderful stories (plays) for the book. Here they are in alphabetical order: Nick Skinner from Abcam, Becky Cody from Ascentis, Kristina Vaneva formerly from Atlantis Resorts, Dominic Price from Atlassian, Helen Cummings from Burton's Biscuit Company, Phil Burgess from C Space, Rosanna Paratschek from Certis Security, Philip Vickers and Sam Shaw from Charles Tyrwhitt, Sara Matthews formerly from Chelsea Football Club, Breckon Jones from Deloitte Australia, Alex Darby from EU Automation, Honor Beattie from Heineken, Roshine Bulpitt from HomeServe, Alex Hirst and Lizzie Penny from Hoxby Collective, Madhulika Chowdhary from InterGlobe Aviation Limited, Samantha Thomas-Berry from Kellogg Company, Janet Hulme from Key Forensic Services, Neil Piper from Kentucky Fried Chicken, Johanna Dickinson and Rachel Ovington from KP Snacks, Katherine Gilbert from LinkedIn, Glenn Grayson from Missguided, Marcus Lamont from NAHL Group plc, Claire Clarke from Nationwide, Patti Cuthill from NextLevel Internet, Matthew Cook from North Construction, Amy Zimmerman from Relay Payments, Catrin Lewis from Reward Gateway, Nebel Crowhurst from Roche Pharmaceuticals, Thomas Dibble from Shell Energy Retail, Jennifer LaFountain from Southern New Hampshire University, Lisa Dolan from Teleperformance, Ian Hodson from University of Lincoln, Libby Watkins from Watford Community Housing, Deirdre Ward formerly from Watford Community Housing, Ryan McGrory from Youi, Martiza Lewis from Zappos, and Lynne Oldham and Beth McLaughlin from Zoom.

Let me also thank Reward Gateway for lending me the best editing team in the world, Chloe Thompson, Meghan Barrett and Liana Moore-

Butler, and the best designer, Leonie Williamson. You all make my words and ideas come to life!

Next, let me thank the authors of those books that I used for my research. If you don't have their books on your reading list, I'd suggest doing so, as they're all great in different ways. Here they are in alphabetical order:

- *1001 Ways to Reward Employees* by Bob Nelson

- *Bring Your Whole Self to Work* by Mike Robbins

- *Build it: The Rebel Playbook for Employee Engagement* by Glenn Elliott and Debra Corey

- *Crave* by Gregg Lederman

- *Drive* by Daniel H. Pink

- *Fear Less: How to Win at Life Without Losing Yourself* by Dr Pippa Grange

- *Leading with Gratitude* by Adrian Gostick and Chester Elton

- *The 5 Languages of Appreciation in the Workplace* by Gary Chapman & Paul White

- *Think Again* by Adam Grant

- *Unleashed* by Frances Frei & Anne Morriss

And finally, I'd like to thank my wonderful husband, Ken Corey. Throughout the months when I was writing this book, he patiently discussed and debated the various topics, sharing his insights as a manager, and constantly pushing and challenging me to present ideas and thoughts that would provoke and inspire change. Your name should really be on the cover along with mine, but don't worry, it's in my heart, and for that I appreciate it and you!